Addressing Atheism

Is Authentic Faith Possible?

Gregory M. Weeks

Copyright ©2018 by Gregory M. Weeks. All rights reserved.

ISBN: 978-0-359-06087-0

Unless otherwise noted, Scripture quotations in this publication are from the Common English Bible. © Copyright 2011 by the Common English Bible. All rights reserved. Used by permission.

Other Scriptures used as noted are:

The AMPLIFIED BIBLE (AMP): Scripture taken from the AMPLIFIED® BIBLE, Copyright © 1954, 1958, 1962, 1964, 1965, 1987 by the Lockman Foundation Used by Permission.

THE MESSAGE: THE BIBLE IN CONTEMPORARY ENGLISH (TM): Scripture taken from THE MESSAGE: THE BIBLE IN CONTEMPORARY ENGLISH, copyright©1993, 1994, 1995, 1996, 2000, 2001, 2002. Used by permission of NavPress Publishing Group.

The New Revised Standard Version Bible (NRSV), copyright © 1989 National Council of the Churches of Christ in the United States of America. Used by permission. All rights reserved.

For Barbara, Cameron and Emma

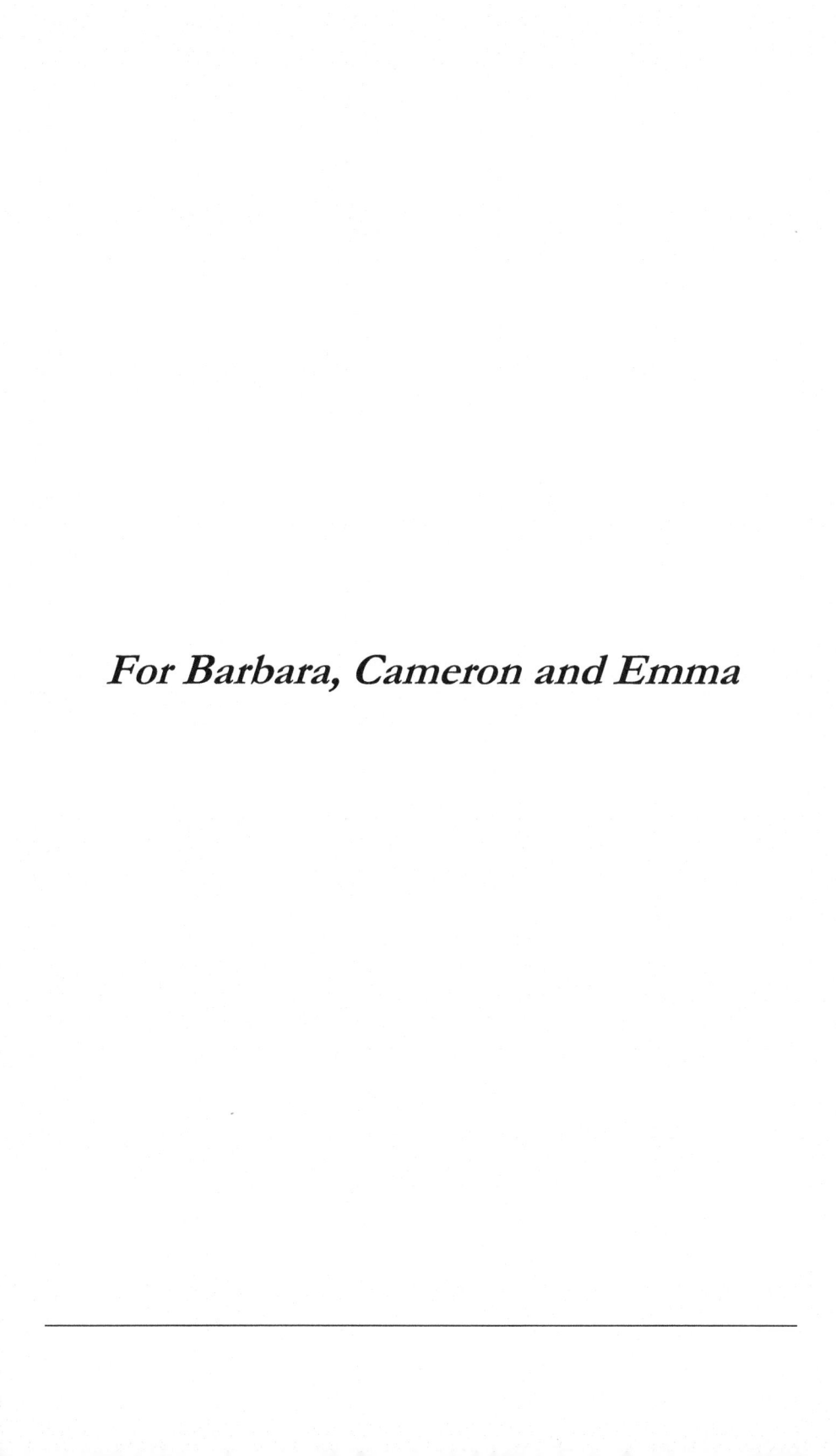

Table of Contents

Preface

Starting the Journey

Introduction (1)

Chapter One—Where Atheists Are Right (7)

Chapter Two—Where Fundamentalists Are Right (13)

Chapter Three—Connecting Atheists and Fundamentalists (19)

Deconstructing

Chapter Four—You Aren't Who You Think You Are (27)

Chapter Five—God Isn't Who You Think God Is (33)

Chapter Six—The Bible Isn't What You Think It Is (37)

Turning

Chapter Seven—Honesty and Humility, In That Order (45)

Chapter Eight—Transcendence and Gratitude (49)

Chapter Nine—Mystery: A Collection of Strange Events (55)

Chapter Ten—Jesus Isn't Who You Think He Is (63)

Reconstructing

Chapter Eleven—Faith Isn't What You Think It Is (73)

Chapter Twelve—The Church Isn't What You Think It Is (77)

Chapter Thirteen—A Different Take on the Bible (85)

Chapter Fourteen—A Different Vision (93)

Chapter Fifteen—A Brief Conclusion (99)

Epilogue—In the Shadow of Mountains (103)

Bibliography (105)

Appendix A (107)

Appendix B (111)

Questions for Reflection and Discussion (113)

Preface

Is authentic faith possible?

The quest for a faith that both makes sense and feels right has been a lifelong personal endeavor. Frankly, I've never been able simply to believe something that defies reason unless there's a good reason for it. At the same time, in my spiritual journey I've bumped up against things that make me question my questions.

Hence the tension, and hence this book.

In reflecting after writing these pages, it strikes me that there really is a fine line between sincere believer and sincere non-believer. We have more in common than we may think as we live out this mystery called life. People who thicken that line may be dealing more with personal issues than with theological ones.

My purpose in this book is to make that line as thin as possible.

It's written for both believer and non-believer alike. It's not meant to convert anybody, although the preacher part of me finds that difficult to write. Rather, honestly, it's meant to be a resource for you wherever you may be in your quest to make sense of things in a way that's authentic to you. Personally, my belief in Jesus is that he understands our limitations and honors spiritual journeys begun with integrity.

One other note.

Since this work is the fruit of a decades-long endeavor, it's sprinkled throughout with some personal experiences. I hope these serve as points for illustration and perhaps spur memories of similar occasions in your life. If some are distractions in your reading, though, I apologize.

Hopefully, regardless of your path in faith/non-faith, this work will prompt reflection and perhaps conversation. I've included some questions at the end that may be helpful for this. Also, check out the bibliography. These are influential works, some of which I'll reference in the chapters ahead. They are an eclectic mix ranging from neuroscience and psychology to theology and sociology.

I'm indebted to many people for help with this project. The members and staff at Manchester United Methodist Church have been very supportive during a summer leave to complete it. Also, people from a variety of backgrounds took time to read and offer *very* helpful insights, without which this couldn't have been accomplished. Among these are Ken Burres, professor of Biblical studies and religion; Hemant Mehta, atheist; Carl Schenck, clergy; Paul Wallace, professor of physics; and Rob Wilson, professor of history. They were very generous with their reflections and suggestions. Thank you all!

Greg Weeks
September, 2018

Starting the Journey

There lives more faith in honest doubt, believe me, than in half the creeds.

--Alfred Lord Tennyson

Introduction

I remember very clearly the first time I lost faith.

It was at the end of my second of three years in seminary. Pastoring a church was on the near horizon. Losing one's faith at that particular time was not a good career move.

Life and death events, however, are no respecter of vocational plans.

Atlanta, summer of 1977.

It was a time for playing tennis in the cut-with-a-knife humidity, then enjoying the sacrament of pizza and frosty drinks with friends.

That was therapy, because the only reason in the world I would swelter in this Georgia sweat lodge was to complete a seminary requirement.

Divinity students sign up to learn about God, the Bible and church, among other things. Clinical Pastoral Education, however, is a course where they discover they must also learn about themselves and life.

So it was that I engaged in this rite of seminary passage that summer. My CPE setting was a children's hospital. More specifically, I was assigned as chaplain to the children struggling in the Intensive Care Unit.

That was just great.

Why not a nice floor like same day surgery or physical therapy or something?

But no.

ICU.

Those three letters are still chilling.

That's the floor housing infants born malformed or premature. Kids of all ages hooked up, Inquisition-like, with needles tubed to bags of multi-colored liquids. Nurses in blue scrubs tended room to room carrying out physicians' orders, physicians who tried to spend as little time possible in situations that appeared hopeless.

Such as in Bobby's case.

Bobby was a twelve-year-old boy with Cystic Fibrosis, an insidious disease that eats away at the respiratory and digestive systems. He had brown hair that fell over his forehead and blue eyes that stared at you with a very knowing gaze.

His father had said that Bobby knew more about life at 12 than he did at 44, because of all the stuff he'd endured in his short existence. He cried relating this as he chain-smoked Marlboros. It seemed as if every parent in the waiting room smoked back then, a heavy cloud of it hanging in the air as we talked.

The child had always been sickly thin, of course. While the other boys played the games of boyhood, Bobby sat on the sidelines. Kids were nice to him, and he to them, but everyone, including Bobby, knew. He was different, and he was probably going to die.

And now here he was, hooked up to IV's in both arms, with a machine rhythmically helping him breathe.

For two weeks I tended to him daily. He quickly became the kid brother I never had. It's possible that a twenty-three-year-old could have a twelve-year-old sibling, and he became mine.

We'd watch cartoons, like the Flintstones, in silence; Bobby couldn't speak because of the breathing apparatus. We ate popsicles, with me feeding him since his arms were pinned to the IV's. I even helped him with bathroom chores, a bit strange in looking back upon it now, but I didn't think twice about it back then. That's what families do.

Finally, inevitably, it came.

On a Saturday night, returning to the house where I rented a sleeping room, the landlady handed me a note. Bobby's parents requested I come to the hospital.

It's absolutely impossible to describe, unless you've been there, the dread-fear-loathing you have in making such a trip. You think of every excuse possible to avoid it, but you can't. It's like going into an MMA cage match against a muscled gladiator who's jeering, "Come on in! Come on in!"

Walking onto the floor, you knew the end was approaching. Nurses no longer had that fake-cheerful demeanor. There's no smiling away the impending death of a child.

The family told me that the doctor was coming to talk to them. We sat and waited. He finally arrived and explained that there was nothing more they could do for Bobby. His lungs were shot and he'd always be hooked to a machine. He explained that they could give him morphine and turn off the mechanism, or just simply let him remain as he was and continue deteriorating.

Tearfully, prayerfully, they made the decision to disconnect.

For two hours we held vigil around his bed. His family reminisced about earlier times, about his mischievousness. His mother stroked his hair as she told him how much she loved him, hoping that somehow, in the morphine unconsciousness, he would hear.

Around two a.m., after some struggle, he sucked in one last breath. Incredibly, as he exhaled, he turned his head toward his mother and opened his eyes.

Gazing at her, he died.

We all did the grieving thing, the crying thing, for a while. I then did the praying thing and excused myself, letting the family be alone.

I remember going out into the dark of the Atlanta early morning and doing something I had never done in my life.

I used every expletive I knew in addressing God.

Actually, I used the biggest expletive of all. I simply gave up believing there could be a God.

No amount of rationalizing could get the deity off the hook for this one. A little boy, my imagined kid brother, who had had no chance in life, gets snuffed out while looking at his mother.

And that's just one kid. How many thousands of times each day is this scene played out around the world, with the innocent being tortured, brutalized, killed?

Believe in a God who would allow this?

Never.

It's been over forty years since I stumbled into that ICU room and thus through the gates of hell. I went ahead and completed seminary. After that, in an eye's blink, I've now finished four decades in ministry, which should tell you that I did regain a semblance of faith.

That faith today, though, is quite a bit different from the one that accompanied me on my rounds as a student chaplain. It's now tougher yet more vulnerable. It's been seasoned by witnessing subsequent tragedies good people endure, things I wouldn't wish on any enemy. My faith has also been conditioned by small groups where people ask honest questions that have no easy answers, let alone absolute ones.

Accordingly, and to this very day, I'm occasionally nagged by a recurring, disturbing thought. "What if, in the midst of all I've trusted and believed, Freud was right?" Religion is just an illusion. It's a drug we take to de-sensitize ourselves to the pain of life and to the ultimate reality of death. The delusion of a caring God is a button we keep pushing to get a hit of a psychological narcotic.

This small book you're reading is a culmination of my lifelong struggle for a faith that makes sense and feels right.

It's geared to those who are honest with their doubts. If your honesty has led you to claim the title "atheist," I respect that, since sincerity is something I strive for as well. In the following pages I simply want to present a perspective on life for you to consider. It's how I have come to believe in God today. Regardless of whether you arrive at the same conclusions, I hope what you read in these pages will help you in the quest we share: to find depth in a world that seems happy to be cascading down a water slide into a shallow pool.

This writing project is also for fellow religious folks. I hope you'll find tools that will assist you in your spiritual journey.

A part of what you'll read came from a sermon series I preached at the amazing parish I've been privileged to serve, Manchester United Methodist. It was a popular series, but not without a bit of controversy. That's because some sacred cows, by necessity, were put out to pasture temporarily. Some listeners (along with this preacher) felt a bit uneasy at times.

The series started, as this book will start, with what I firmly believe. **The root of faith grows best in the soil of honest questioning**. Doubt is the great equalizer of humanity. No matter how pious or impious we may be, our fate in life is to be confronted by mysteries of existence we will never comprehend. From skeptic to believer, we're all throwing darts in the dark, hoping to hit a bullseye we'll never clearly see.

For some, it's just too scary to face the world without the shield of doctrine. Questioning creeds is more than an intellectual exercise for them. It's an existential one. If you question God's existence, or if Jesus is the only way, or if God's Word is infallible, you're getting too close to the edge.

This might lead to uncomfortableness in some religious folks in reading the "deconstructing" section of this book. For the record, I felt uncomfortable writing it. Yet, how will existing faith grow unless we're honest about things? And how will any who don't believe in God ever develop an authentic faith unless we dare look at the world through clear, not rosy, lenses?

Medieval maps, in noting uncharted areas, tacked on the warning, "Here there be dragons." In conventional religion, if you question too much, you could find yourself expelled into that dragon-infested wasteland.

Those dragons, though, might end up being friendly. They might respect brave travelers. Uncharted territory can yield surprises in a good way. For some it may lead to a faith that's more authentic to who they are, their experiences, their thoughts. For others it may return them to the church, but with different vision. They won't settle for mainstream wisdom but will keep pushing the envelope. They will see old things in new ways.

One of those "things" is Jesus. It's my hope that by the end of this book, he'll appear a lot less unbelievable-distant-holy and a lot more human-alive-approachable. It's my hope his church will appear a lot less stuffy and a lot more open; after all, it should be a place where his personality shines through. I also hope that the Bible will appear a lot less irrelevant and a lot more interesting and inviting.

All of this will eventually bring us to the final point of viewing our world a bit differently. Doing some interior work (spoiler alert: it entails honesty and humility) may shift our outlook a few degrees. Some priorities and relationships may be altered. If you happen to find yourself changed in some small way by the time you finish reading, then you will cope by trying to change the world in some small way. Ultimately, faith comes from action, and action deepens faith.

It's also my hope that there will be another, and somewhat unexpected, payoff from tilling this soil.

If we journey together in these pages, perhaps by the end we will share a profound discomfort with the divisiveness driving our current culture. The process of searching for faith is a process of inquisitive openness. That's counter to the trend of retreating behind party lines and shouting/tweeting slogans and insults.

Simply put, if you're able to become more open to God (or whatever you might call the Mystery), then you will automatically become more open to a diverse yet connected humanity.

Chapter One—*Where Atheists Are Right*

From the traditional church perspective, "atheist" is not exactly a term of endearment. It conjures a variety of unfortunate stereotypes. An atheist is someone who's angry, cynical and pessimistic. Or someone who is anti-God and anti-church. Or someone without good values and morals.

Perhaps part of this comes from voices of some popular atheists. Richard Dawkins, Christopher Hitchens and Sam Harris have taken a hostile stance, along the lines of the only good religion is an extinct one. The title of Hitchens' book, *God Is Not Great: How Religion Poisons Everything*, rather sums things up.

It's not accurate to lump all atheists together, however. It would be like lumping together all Christians; one size, or one label, doesn't fit all. To portray all non-believers as angry does an injustice to those who may have considered faith but simply find it lacking. It also inhibits dialogue between believers/non-believers that could be beneficial to both sides.

To get a more balanced picture of modern atheism, I would suggest reading the writings of Hemant Mehta. He is a young self-avowed atheist who blogs on a website with the intriguing title, "The Friendly Atheist." He's also written *I Sold My Soul on E-Bay*, a book chronicling his adventures in attending a variety of churches. His open-minded approach, honesty and humor should prick any prejudicial view of an atheist. (Additionally, his book offers helpful insights to church folks from an outsider's point of view.)

There's an easy summary for why people don't believe in God. It doesn't make any sense.

<u>Freud</u> argued that God is simply a projection of our need for an Invisible Daddy in the sky. Og the caveman needed protection from the mastodon, and Sue needs healing from cancer: the belief in God comes in handy. God is an imaginary deity existing only in our minds.

Accordingly, as we've become more sophisticated, knowledgeable and technologically savvy, do we really need divine protection (that is, of course, other than at final exam time)? Moreover, do we really need God in order to be nice to each other? You don't need a belief in order to protect your buddy in combat or fill a sandbag for a neighbor during a flood or run a food drive at Christmas time.

<u>Marx</u> argued against God in political terms. The concept of the deity is an invention by powerful people in order to protect their interests and solidify their standing. Religion is a drug administered to the masses in order to keep them in line. God is also used to stoke the sick agenda of religious extremists who justify driving planes into buildings, then partying while they see the flames.

<u>Rationalists</u> argue that this world, for all its complexity and wonder, is still flawed. If you're going to build a house, why build one with holes in the roof and a leaky foundation? How can I defend God when I see things happening in the world that I, if I were God, would never allow to happen? I wouldn't let children be born with hideous diseases nor be raised in environments where gruesome things happen. Yet diseases with unpronounceable names still ravage and destroy young lives before they have a chance, and children are still abused, maimed and manipulated (sometimes in the name of God).

Evolution explains things in a cleaner, clearer way.

What's more, given the enormity and complexity of life, does it at all make sense that there could be an invisible deity that randomly appears here and there, contravening natural laws, then disappears until another God-in-the-box popup? And isn't it also a complete stretch of credulity to think that such a being could catalogue the number of hairs on your head (Matthew 10:30), even though you're only one of over seven billion humans occupying this planet?

Speaking of God popping up here and there…why aren't there objective demonstrations of God's supernatural existence? Jesus supposedly did some of those demonstrations. You can't get more supernatural than raising someone from the dead. But outside of "The Walking Dead," where do you see such things today? If God wanted you to believe, then wouldn't God have made it a lot easier for you to do so? Many of the Biblical characters who saw miracles had little trouble believing in God. But where are those signs now? Consequently, it makes you think that the Biblical stuff was made up.

If you could, by some mental manipulation, believe in the existence of such a super power, then what does such a being look like? Let's go back to the time when God supposedly popped up a lot.

Even though we'll look more closely at the Bible later, it's worth noting here that the portrait of God painted in these pages can display a few odd, offensive brushstrokes.

God commands the Hebrews to utterly destroy men, women and children in the land they're about to invade. They are to show absolutely "no pity" (Deuteronomy 7:16; 1 Samuel 15:1-3). And this is a God of love?

God strikes down a man who's trying to keep the Ark of the Covenant from falling and getting damaged. His crime? He didn't have the proper authority to touch it (2 Samuel 6:1-7; 1 Chronicles 13:9-12). His death possibly resulted in him leaving a widow who had no means of support and children who would now have no father. And this is a God of love and patience?

God makes a couple of bets with Satan that result in a righteous, faithful man named Job losing his family, wealth and health (Job 1:12, 2:6). And this is a God of love, patience and justice?

So, for the non-believer, the divine portrait isn't exactly a Rembrandt. The late comedian George Carlin saw the humor of it all. His religion bit (YouTube "George Carlin on Religion and God") presented his viewpoint, profanely, in just over a minute. There's an invisible Man in the sky taking note of what you do daily, keeping a list. If you fail, He will send you to spend an eternity in hell, writhing and screaming and crying. BUT, He loves you, and needs money.

George had a way of getting right to the point.

He was also angry with the religious establishment that would promote, and profit from, this imaginary deity.

Just as it's easy to make unfortunate stereotypes of atheists, so is it easy to do so with believers.

Three religious caricatures come to mind, fueling atheistic fire.

SMUG EXCLUSIVISTS

Occasionally I'll preach a sermon about Christianity and other religions. I'll talk about Dave Kornblum, the man who befriended my dad when my mother was dying from cancer. Dave opened up his house to him, fed him, listened to him and helped him cry. I'll say how "Kornblum" isn't exactly an Irish name. He was a Jew. And I'll conclude by asking, "Do you honestly think that God will send a compassionate man like Dave to hell because he wasn't a Christian?"

I'll conclude with, "No! God is bigger than that. Dave is NOT in hell." I'll then add a quote attributed to the late Archbishop of Brazil, Dom Helder Camara: "In the Father's house we shall meet Buddhists and Jews, Moslems and Protestants - even a few Catholics too, I dare say."

A few parishioners will thank me, because they'd been abused by ultra-religious people advocating "turn or burn." Such folk scissor one verse ("I am the way...no one comes to the Father but through me" John 14:6) and take this as the platform from which to exclude others from salvation. It's unfortunate that the louder someone pounds the pulpit, the easier it is to believe the stereotype is the norm.

UPTIGHT PIETISTS

Historically, Christians have had a lot of hang-ups about a lot of things.

They've had all sorts of problems with sex. No sex before marriage or outside of marriage. How you define "having sex" is up for grabs, but they've emphasized how dangerous it is nonetheless.

Furthermore, any expression of sexuality that begins with something other than "hetero" has been labeled sinful.

There are other sins as well, according to a variety of traditions. Gambling, alcohol and drugs are almost as big as the sex prohibition. Lesser transgressions have historically included card playing, movies, pinball machines, dancing, rock music, Halloween, short skirts, magic, feminism, Eastern meditation/yoga, video games, tattooing, cursing and smoking.

If people believe that Christian standard bearers are people like this, quick to judge and point a self-righteous finger at an evil horde of video gamers, then no wonder they stay away from church on a Sunday morning.

Which is another sin, by the way.

EMOTIONALLY MANIPULABLE

I was serving as a chaplain at a hospital and visiting an older woman who was angry. Very angry. She was mad that the doctors hadn't helped her, healed her, made her feel better. She railed on them for a while, then stopped and got real serious.

"You know, if those doctors don't do me any good, I'm going to go to a faith healer. He'll do the job."

Why, of course. If you can't get what you want from the medical profession, get it from the faith healers. Do whatever they say, amble down front, and receive a blessing.

This seems somewhat similar, in my opinion, to what Martin Luther condemned 500 years ago in the Catholic church regarding a practice called indulgences. You are concerned about a loved one in purgatory? No problem. Give the priest some money and your fun-loving Uncle Josh will spend less time atoning for his sins. It's about what you need from God, and what God wants you to do to get it.

I hope the vulnerable people who believe such things will receive help and comfort in some fashion. However, they feed into the stereotype that these are the folks who gravitate toward religion. They are prone to believe religious professionals promising their heart's desire if they only have enough faith, and perhaps also make a nice donation.

I believe that most atheists know very well that ordinary, normal everyday people can sincerely believe in God without falling into any of the above exaggerated categories. They don't share Carlin's angst.

Yet the point is that some religious types use their belief in God as an outlet to speak and act in ways that may be contrary to "love thy neighbor." This, added to the rational reasons for unbelief, is further justification to dump the whole religion thing, God included.

I wrote a column for a local newspaper regarding how people who don't believe in God and people who do should relate to one another. I stressed (spoiler alert again) humility and honesty from both sides.

I thought it was a rather pleasant article, along the lines of inviting both sides to have cookies and milk together. However, at least one person didn't understand it that way. Their comment:

> I can't help but think that [this] is the obvious position religion is facing now and increasingly so in the future. When it's clear you're going to lose the war, it's best to be nice and negotiate as good a deal as you can to allow you to survive as long as you can.
>
> While I can appreciate the olive branch, the sooner religion vanishes, the better. There's no room for religion at the table of the future. You can help speed this up by not participating in the immoral practice of inculcating children with religious dogma.

I take such a reaction as being from a fringe group of non-believers you wouldn't want to invite to a party. The hostile response to an invitation to dialogue, though, makes you wonder.

Such anger may mask deeper issues. The intensity of that emotion is shared by some folks in a totally different camp.

The fundamentalists.

Chapter Two—*Where Fundamentalists Are Right*

If there are different camps within atheism, there are different battalions within Christianity.

There is such a potpourri of Jesus followers that you wonder if they believe in the same Christ.

New Testament scholar Marcus Borg, in his book *Convictions*, suggested dividing Christians into five types: conservative, conventional, uncertain, former and progressive. There are sub-divisions within these types. Comprising the conservative ranks are fundamentalists, conservative-evangelicals and some mainline Protestant/Catholics.

I want to focus on fundamentalism, while acknowledging the limitation in so doing.

Strict fundamentalists, as I'll describe below, are a Christian minority. They are a very visible minority and, unfortunately, easy to caricature. It is not accurate to depict them as mainline conservative-evangelical.

For this book, though, they serve as a useful stark contrast to rational atheists. Their extremism helps us clarify religious issues, so we can begin the conversation. Their beliefs are easy, simple and straightforward. They believe what they believe, period. No apology or explanation needed.

Additionally, I empathize greatly with this theological company within the conservative Christian platoon. It's how I started out, and it makes sense.

At 15 I had a deeply moving religious experience. I had read some passages in the New Testament and was convinced. I asked Jesus to forgive all my adolescent sinning. When I did, my guilt lifted. Jesus, whom I had called upon, put an arm around my shoulder and said, basically, "It's on me now. You're forgiven!"

When you're a teenager, there's hot or cold, no lukewarm. I threw myself into following this Jesus who had suddenly become personal.

In the process, I came to one fundamental realization.

Since reading the Bible revealed the path to Jesus, then it is to be held sacred at all costs. After all, God is perfect and such a God wouldn't give us an imperfect book about Himself.

Ergo, the Bible is perfect.

Given this fact, the most important thing we Christians can do is to look at life through the Bible's eyes. That is where we find salvation, God's will, and all other things Christian.

From this starting point, five fundamentals of faith emerge.

1. The Bible is literally infallible, at least in its original transmission. Pretty simple there.
2. Jesus is the Son of God. All those creedal formulations, like the Nicene Creed (Jesus "is begotten from the Father before all ages"), are true and must be defended.
3. Jesus was born of a virgin. This is foretold in the Old Testament. If Isaiah and Luke said it, that settles it.
4. Jesus bore our sins on the cross. That's how the cross saves us. Jesus paid it all. There's a fountain filled with blood and, if dipped in it, we'll become white as snow.
5. Jesus was physically resurrected and will return to judge the earth. We must be vigilant and ready. Could happen any time.

Once you start from where a fundamentalist starts, you proceed down a road that is very straight, with few dips or curves.

If the Bible is perfect, then you must trust it before you trust your own reason. After all, we're sinners stained by original sin, which blurs our judgment. You must therefore study the Word thoroughly and carefully. This reading also comes with the assumption that if you don't understand something, it's your problem and not God's or the Bible's.

When you study it this way, some things become very clear.

There's pain and suffering in the world because of our sin. The problem of Bobby's death in the Introduction is solved. A child's death doesn't feel right, but feelings are secondary. In Adam's transgression we all sinned and messed everything up. That's why parental sins are visited upon their children and grandchildren, great-grandchildren, and great-great grandchildren. It's in the Bible (Exodus 20:5, 34:7).

Ethics are clear.

Women are to have a subordinate role to men (Ephesians 5:22-24; Colossians 3:18). They should be quietly respectful, since men bear the likeness of Christ. They're an afterthought, after all (Genesis 2:21-23).

Anything but heterosexual relations is a sin (Romans 1:24-25, for example). Also, sex is for reproduction (Genesis 1:28).

Divorce is a sin and not to be tolerated, except in adulterous cases (Malachi 2:16; Matthew 5:32). Consequently, abuse is not a reason for divorce, so a spouse must stay in such a marriage. Maybe by her diligence she will save her husband (1 Peter 3:1-2). This may not feel right in some cases but, once again, feelings are secondary. It's in the Bible.

Child-rearing is a strict matter and corporal punishment is appropriate where and when needed. Spare that rod and you'll spoil that child (a paraphrase of Proverbs 13:24).

Science is as clear as ethics.

Genesis is fact, since it's in the Bible. The detail that modern science, including evolution, refutes Genesis 1-3 is inconsequential. Scientific data is flawed because such data comes from humans and humans are flawed. Perhaps it's a trick of Satan, to make us question the truth of the Bible. Again, the Bible is the authority, not Darwin.

Fundamentalist authors and apologists spend much energy in finding ways to present evidence for their claims.

There's a movement within some fundamentalist circles to give an alt-science response to mainstream science's objection to literal Biblical claims. Thus is Ken Ham's famous Creation Museum in Kentucky that takes on the fake-science news. He marshals facts to prove the scientific validity of Genesis. The statement on the museum's website crystallizes the fundamentalist's viewpoint: "When you start with the Bible as your ultimate authority, you're ready to discover creation science."

This drives such scholars as Bill Nye, the Science Guy, absolutely crazy. He wrote a book where he rebutted creation science, titling it, *Undeniable: Evolution and the Science of Creation*. He goes into elaborate detail explaining the origins of evolution and the facts behind it. He also throws in details about the age of the universe and of the dinosaurs. This does not deter Mr. Ham and his followers. The Bible trumps even a smart guy like Bill Nye. It could be that, alliteratively speaking, secular science is subject to Satan.

In addition to creation science, fundamentalists turn to movies to press the attack against the devil. The "Left Behind" series is based on a literal interpretation of the last book of the Bible, Revelation. That book contains graphic images of the end of the world, complete with the Antichrist (#666) and Jesus coming back to rescue his own while everyone else is left to the mercies of Satan. It's a symbolic book, written to strengthen early Christians during persecution. Taken literally, though, it's a nice complement to Genesis. God created. God punishes. Get your life together and believe in Jesus while there's still time.

More recent are the "God's Not Dead" films. Atheists are often presented as bad, mean, misguided, wicked pawns of the devil. They really want to prove that God is dead, once and for all. Christians are good, gentle, insightful and righteous. They speak up for God, and God vindicates them just as Daniel was vindicated in the lion's den.

As fundamentalists fervently and sincerely defend their faith, they also put that faith into action.

"Secular humanism" appears to be on the rise, with the tolerance of multiple religions, the legalization of same-sex marriage, the anti-discrimination laws protecting the LGBTQ community and the tolerance of abortion. This is an affront to the Christian values they see in the Bible. Their only way to counter this is to vote the correct candidates into office. Consequently, right-wing Christianity marries right-wing politics.

This righteous anger isn't limited to a fallen society, however.

Christians who support some of the above causes may be in their crosshairs as well. At least the humanists are just ignorant of the Gospel. But believers who advocate things that are against God's Word? That's a greater sin. If voting the correct candidates in is the fundamentalists' answer to secular humanism, then distancing themselves from apostasy is their response to such misguided souls. This is why we have lots of churches.

On a more positive note, those in the ultra-conservative camp can be the most creative in reaching out to others. Since they have a sincere desire to save souls from hell, they will passionately and creatively witness, through both words and actions. Their care and love are genuine. Even though you may not agree with them, their fervor is exemplary.

Thus is the world of the fundamentalists, from my perspective.

They are right, given their assumption that believing the purity of the Bible directly correlates to believing in the existence of God. They are to be admired for holding on to that assumption in the face of strong criticism and arguments.

But what about those who would consider themselves simply "conservative-evangelicals?" They would not go to such extreme measures as these far-right believers. They wouldn't buy tickets to the

Creation Museum because they believe there's a way to hold Biblical truth and scientific truth together. They don't have to be enemies.

These sincere believers make up the majority of the conservative fold. They are more open-minded and willing to dialogue freely regarding issues. They are deeply devoted to Christ and will express Christ's love in sincere, non-judgmental ways. They can enjoy life in a more relaxed, less uptight, manner.

Such folks may face some challenges, though, when it comes to the Bible.

If you say that perhaps the Bible isn't literally infallible, and perhaps some things are symbolic/mythological and not historic fact, you start sliding down a slope with a questionable braking mechanism.

You may try to reconcile things that can't be reconciled. "Those seven days of creation weren't literally twenty-four hour days. They were like millions of years."

You'll use the reason, "The Bible was infallible in its earliest form, and some parts might be corrupted in subsequent translations." Perhaps this would explain such weird places where male angels mate with female humans to produce a race of giants (Genesis 6:1-4).

You'll look for explanations for miracles. "When Jesus multiplied the loaves and fishes to feed five thousand people (Mark 6:35-44), what really happened was that he inspired them to start sharing with each other."

Additionally, since some Biblical laws affront our modern sensitivities, conservative-evangelicals will relax a few of the restrictions in the name of Christian love. Loosen the prohibition on divorce, so a spouse can escape an abusive relationship. Let women speak in church, since they are equal to men. Work on the Sabbath, since there's a lot of competition and God would understand.

But when you start relaxing rules, what's your basis, and how do you choose? It may be difficult distinguishing between God's will and personal bias. Slavery was in the "justified by the Bible" category, and it took a war to overturn that verdict. Homosexuality is currently being debated, and some denominations are going through a civil war of their own.

Given the difficulty of trying to be consistent in reverence for the Bible, some conservatives will admit there is difficulty in understanding some things in Scripture. However, since God's Word is true, they will accept it on faith and trust. Reconciling the Bible to modern thinking is impossible for humanity, but all things are possible for God.

Such a default setting respects the Bible. It shows appropriate deference since it's through Holy Scripture we can encounter God.

While this stance works for the faithful, it will be a turnoff for others. It's akin to, "Well, just have faith in the Bible and you'll find faith in God." This comes across as a mandate to stop thinking critically and honestly if you want to believe.

The conservative-evangelicals may, then, live in tension between an ancient book revered as sacred and a modern mindset that simply rebels at some of the anomalies and assertions found in it.

The fundamentalists free themselves from such stress. They are a lot more clear-cut, "here's where I stand, take it or leave it," in their faith. They are consistent. The Bible said it. Case closed.

There's a lot to be said for such clarity and consistency.

One of the things to be said is that there may be a unique connection between atheist and fundamentalist.

Chapter Three—*Connecting Atheists and Fundamentalists*

On the surface, atheist and fundamentalist are poles apart. If one were to debate the other, the result would be further entrenchment in their respective positions. No one would convince the other because minds are already made up. A debate would only produce anger that the other side is so oblivious to the obvious truth.

Yet, both fervent believer/non-believer are much more alike than either would want to admit.

In the next chapter we're going to delve into the puzzle of the human brain as it relates to this. Right now, it's important to note two things about our minds.

One is the strong, unconscious need that internally drives us. Like a self-driving car, our brain is a complex machine running an automatic program that will deliver us to our destination of security, consistency and identity.

Regarding <u>security</u>, we all need a mindset that makes the world understandable and controllable. It is, after all, a terrifying place. We grow up and see parents, siblings and friends die. We get sick because of invisible bugs. Tornadoes slam our homes in the South and Midwest, and hurricanes blow us away in the Caribbean.

Everything is unpredictable. Life is fine one moment and we're orphans the next.

The older we grow, the more we need a mindset that tames this world. We need something that makes this frightening place less scary and confusing.

Some of us seek emotional peace through faith. Freud was indeed right that faith in God gives us this edge on life.

Some of us might find such inner peace by some other philosophy, such as rationalism, science and the empirical method.

Regardless, we need a mindset that makes us feel secure.

Psychologist Abraham Maslow, in the middle of the last century, developed his famous "hierarchy of needs," which looks like a big pyramid. At the top are the needs of love, belonging and self-actualization. However, you can never ascend to that level if you're looking over your shoulder all the time.

An outlook on life that gives you a sense of control and predictability is vital. It's a big part of the pyramid's base.

Once your brain has claimed that mindset, it will do whatever it can to make it <u>consistent</u>.

Academic psychologist Rob Brotherton explored why some people believe outlandish theories ("Was the moon landing faked?"). He notes that people shape their outlook on life so it's consistent. We don't like disorder and conflict; it's unsettling, disruptive. Consequently, we'll make sure our belief system is reliable. If an idea or event threatens that unified wholeness, we'll rationalize it away or simply ignore it. (*Suspicious Minds: Why We Believe Conspiracy Theories*)

As we develop this consistent, coherent world view that makes us feel secure, we seek out people who share it with us. People who think like us are safe and fairly predictable. They support us, and we support them, against outsiders. We learn from each other, further embedding us in our beliefs. This has been going on since we crawled out of the sea. Journalist Sebastian Junger traces this history, emphasizing the importance of <u>identifying</u> with your group. He states that such identification promotes "the eternal quest for meaning." (*Tribe: On Homecoming and Belonging*)

When I met Jesus, for example, everything fell into place. I had a belief system that had millennia of consistent polishing, sustained by a community of people, young and old, who believed like I did. What's more, I had direction for my whole life. I wanted to learn more about Jesus. I wanted to study the Bible. I wanted to put his teachings into practice.

I need such a religious framework. My modus operandi in pastoral life is to begin the morning with a stiff cup of coffee, dive into the Bible and other texts, do some reflecting, and come up with a sermon on an issue that's passionate or relevant. No doubt when I'm in the dying process, if I have a chance, I'll be reflecting on some of those scriptures that mean so much and sing some songs of Zion to provide comfort as I prepare to cross the chilly Jordan.

My faith helps tame the world that's bloody in tooth and claw.

However, a person's lack of faith can do the same thing.

The atheist has a belief system based on the rational.

The world runs on common sense laws that help us understand, predict and prevent things. We live in a big place with mysteries we may not yet comprehend as yet. This doesn't mean, however, that there is some deity just because we haven't figured it out yet. What's important is what we understand now and how we can use that for the betterment of humanity.

Could God have created things? Who cares? We don't see God, nor signs that God exists. We do, though, see a wonderful world that's put together in ways we can decipher and use. Additionally, there are people who think and feel like we do. We get community from them, just as we would from a church.

Together with these like-minded friends, we experience the wonderful freedom that comes from breaking away from the neuroses of religion. John Lennon was right. If we imagine a world without religion, heaven, hell, etc., then we are free to focus just on each other. That's all we have in life, one another, so let's concentrate on that. Enough bad stuff has been done in the name of an imaginary God. Let's just tend to our fellow humans; that's a tribal thing to do instilled in our genes, after all, and we'll all enjoy a wonderful life.

When we die, well, we die. We'll simply cease consciousness. That makes this life all the more important, and relationships in this life all the more vital. It'd be nice to think we keep living in some fashion. Hope is fine, like kids hoping for Santa Claus. But since we can't know for sure, why bother?

It doesn't make sense that we would want to mess things up by imagining a God who doesn't fit in a natural world. If anything, such a capricious God makes the world more, not less, unpredictable. Part of that unpredictability could also be people who do unhealthy, sick things in His name.

If I'm an atheist, I'm going to cling to this mindset as fervently as a Christian clings to John 3:16.

Based on this, I think it's fairly safe to say that atheist and fundamentalist have something in common on the foundational level. They, and we, need a framework to make this world less threatening.

For the believer, that security is a belief system that subjugates reason.

For the atheist, that security is a rationality that excludes faith.
Security is security. Welcome to the human race.

And once they, and we, tame the frightening side of life by buying into a certain outlook that gives us security, consistency and identity, we naturally want to safeguard that perspective.

That's the second interesting point about the brain.

Once our mind has implemented that self-driving program leading to our emotional well-being, it will then do whatever it takes to support and perfect it.

Neuroscientist David Eagleman described the varied levels of our cognitive processes in his book, *Incognito: The Secret Lives of the Brain*. He notes that many processes are happening all the time in our brains. We're unaware of them, but they are all working for our welfare. One of the fascinating things the brain does, in protecting us, is to invent stories. He states that when one part of our brain settles on something, then other parts are quick to invent a story to support that choice.

To the outside observer, these stories may be patently silly. They may appear to have no basis in factual reality. But to the person whose brain has created them, they're as important as oxygen and cheeseburgers.

The fundamentalist grabs onto the story that Jesus saved her from sin and changed her life. There is a loving, and sometimes judging, God. This Father gives her clear instructions, bolsters her belief by giving her a community of faith, and will give her eternal life. She will live her life weaving an on-going narrative based on such assumptions.

The atheist lives by the story that the notion of God doesn't make sense at all and can perpetuate a lot of evil, so life is better by celebrating the advances we can make in science and technology and using our knowledge to make an improved life for all. Like the fundamentalist, he will hear his brain writing continuing episodes based on what he believes to be true.

Two divergent stories, each adopted and adapted by our amazing brain, which works as our great protector.

What's more, since these narratives are so important, your brain is going to focus on those things that will support your story and exclude those things that don't. In law enforcement this is called "confirmation bias." If a detective is sold on a theory, then that officer may unconsciously look for things that confirm what he wants to be true.

So will religious and non-religious people, alike. I'm most naturally going to read things and talk to people who agree with my storyline. I'm going to argue with and resist people who don't.

We thus have a lot of difficulty trying just to get along. Our stories are too precious to us and we don't want them threatened by thinking that the other side might have a narrative that has some truth that contradicts ours. We want the plot to continue smoothly and not get wrenched off course by some new eccentric character introduced in chapter 13.

We grow uncomfortable if we come too close to someone with a different outlook. Our minds invent reasons why they are misguided. We may ask them questions, but not necessarily for clarification. Rather, we're listening for answers to which we can object.

After an exchange that gets nowhere, and perhaps grows a little heated, you either leave or change the subject.

Your inner narrative gives you a sense of safety. When it's challenged, you respond emotionally. You may not really be hearing what the other person is saying because your inner writer has sounded the alarm. It has begun rationalizing to support and defend your narrative.

It would be eye-opening to write down what your inner Hemingway dictates. What are your beliefs, hung together in a consistent pattern supported by people you like, that ground you in life? How strongly do you hold onto them?

The stories we create are invaluable.

Unfortunately, they're also flawed.

Deconstructing

It vexes me when they would constrain science by the authority of the Scriptures, and yet do not consider themselves bound to answer reason and experiment.

--Galileo

Chapter Four—*You Aren't Who You Think You Are*

How often have you had a dream where you're falling? Or one where you find yourself taking a final exam in a class you didn't know you had?

Dreams like these are your brain's way of saying that it doesn't like it when you find yourself out of control. You're scared and vulnerable. Consequently, the brain will do everything possible to keep you out of such unnerving circumstances.

This amazing three-pound mass in our craniums takes us for a rollercoaster ride while we think we're standing still. This is a fact easily summed up:

We are not in control of our mind; our mind controls us.

It is always active, always seeking to make sense of things. It processes things unconsciously based on sight cues and past experiences.

We already saw this in the last chapter when we understood our brains to be great storytellers. They write our storyline in order to fulfill basic needs. They then tie it together with plot and character, and constantly read chapter after chapter to us.

But there are other ways to show the constant and sometimes frantic activity of the brain.

Neuroscientists point to optical illusions, like the one below.

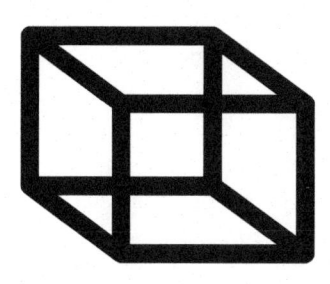

You will see a 3-D cube. Depending on how long you stare at it, it will flip perspective. It will appear as a cube angling downward sometimes and angling upward at other times. You can't see both simultaneously

In reality, though, there is no cube at all. The diagram is just lines drawn on a flat surface.

It's that brain of ours, constantly trying to make sense of things. It layers meaning and perception onto those lines. We can't stop the brain from doing this anymore than we can stop our hearts from beating and our lungs from breathing.

Another example of our brain's frenetic activity is when you attempt to quiet it. Have you tried to simply think of nothing for a few minutes? It might work for a few seconds. Then a little voice inside your head blurts out, "Remember to pick up coffee tonight." It can only remain silent for so long.

Truly, our brains have a mind of their own, always looking after us.

Psychology has labeled this part of our mind the subconscious. It's impossible to overestimate its power.

We may think the conscious part of the brain, what you're using to understand these words, is in control. Our subconscious just lets us believe that deception.

Some modern writers have come up with graphic images to illustrate this.

Eagleman has described the conscious part of our brain as a stowaway on a large ocean liner, the machinery of which is the subconscious. We can run up and down the deck, but the boat is going where it's programmed to go. (*Incognito*)

Brotherton has described our conscious mind as a puppet being controlled by the puppet master subconscious, which is pulling all our strings. We may think we're in charge, but we're really at the master's mercy. (*Suspicious Minds*)

Social psychologist Jonathan Haidt has described our conscious mind as the rider on a big elephant, which is the subconscious. We can shout as many orders as we want, but that elephant is going to do what it wants to do. (*The Happiness Hypothesis*)

While we can work on training this subconscious part of us through study, meditation, etc., it's still going to act on our behalf as best it can. It will color what we see and hear, then prompt us to act, speak and believe, accordingly.

Our rational, conscious mind simply isn't in charge.

What's more, this wet computer in our heads runs programs that have pre-set routines.

There's a genetic influence on our personalities. We have certain tendencies. You naturally lean toward introversion or extroversion and toward being a fact-oriented person or a feeling-oriented one. You can't wake up one morning and say, "I think I'll be an extrovert today," when you're the happiest sitting behind a corner desk in a CPA's office. You're going to perceive the world through your personality defaults.

Also, our brains have a tendency to gravitate toward various moral values. We naturally put more emphasis on some than on others. Once our subconscious grabs onto what it thinks is morally right, then that truth becomes intuitive and beyond question. You'll judge everything from that sacrosanct perspective.

In Jonathan Haidt's *The Righteous Mind*, the psychologist measured such values as care, fairness, loyalty, authority, sanctity and liberty. "Liberals" intuitively put an emphasis upon some of those, while "conservatives" emphasized others. Each group felt it was right and the other wrong. They couldn't understand, like atheists arguing with fundamentalists, why the other side just didn't get it. Their brains had told them they were standing on the truth corner, and not to budge an inch from their righteous position. Thus the subtitle for his book: *Why Good People Are Divided by Politics and Religion*

While we're seeing how our brain isn't a sterling example of clean, unbiased computing, let's throw in our ancestor baggage.

Anyone who does the DNA ancestry thing will get back interesting results. How does your heritage affect how you perceive things and how you act? My mix of British/Irish predispose me to physiological, and I would presume psychological, traits. (We're not even going to talk about the small bit of Neanderthal I have in me which, according to my wife, explains quite a bit.)

Finally, our brains change organically over time and we're not even aware of it.

As young adults we're quick to grasp things in clear-cut terms, black and white. Then after a few decades you look back and wonder, "What in the world was I thinking when I did that?" It's like you're looking at another person, who happened to have a young model of your body, without the aches and funny noises you now have. Then, when you find yourself on the downward slope and your brain starts shrinking, your understanding of what's true and important changes once again.

All of the above paints a clear picture. Our brains are not a computer-clean motherboard objectively receiving data, crunching it and spitting out pristine solutions to life's puzzles. Our brains do not listen to our conscious instructions and submissively obey. Our brains are time-dependent organisms resembling a mish-mash of strung together processing chips running a buggy program, all the while informing us that we are the center of the universe and if people would just think as we do, the world would be a better place.

Our brain is our biggest friend and our greatest deceiver. It runs the program and tells us why we should believe in God or why we shouldn't, all based on giving us security.

The irony is that the biggest deception our brains pull off is the illusion that each of us is important enough to begin with.

Let's put that to rest.

The universe is unimaginably vast, complex and beyond comprehension. We're invisible specks along for the ride.

Look at our tiny solar system.

According to one source (*Today in the Word*, July, 1990), if we were to shrink our sun down from 865,000 miles in diameter to 2 feet, about the size of a beach ball, then our earth would be the size of a pea.

This pea is 220 steps out from the sun. To reach Mars, you would have to walk another 108 steps. To reach Neptune from Mars, you have to walk another 6,130 steps. We haven't even gotten to Pluto. When we did, we would have to walk another 6,720 miles to reach the nearest star in our galaxy.

One of the deep-space shots from the Hubble Space Telescope captured what's thought to be the most distant object ever seen. You see a loner galaxy, a fuzzy red dot in the picture with no other galaxies around it. It's estimated to be at a distance of 31.5 BILLION light years. One light year equals 5,878,499,414,210 miles. So, this galaxy is: 185,172,731,547,615,000,000,000 miles from our insignificant home planet. By the time you're reading this, you should add a few more trillion as it continues its outward journey towards…?
(https://www.wired.com/2011/12/universe-size/)

And if you think THAT is amazing, take a look at something a little closer to home.

The sea turtle.

These turtles will swim hundreds of miles from where they're hatched. They'll cruise the oceans for months. But then, when it's time to lay their eggs, they will return to that very same tiny strand of beach where they themselves were born.

How in the world can they navigate back to the beach? They have no visible landmarks, since their eyes are only able to see a few inches above the surface at best. They have never taken classes in astronomy to determine which direction is due north. The best verdict scientists can give, once they've speculated a theory or two, is this: "It's a mystery."

Well, yeah. On this earth, we have millions of mysteries we'll probably never understand.

Even the mystery of how your own eyeball, reading this description of the turtle, uses its thousands of rods and cones to transmit color and shape to your brain, which then mysteriously processes the words and conjures up an image of a sea turtle, doing this instantaneously without conscious thought, while you continue reading this paragraph and making sense of it: once again, mind *blown*.

What does all this mean?

ANY PRONOUNCEMENT ANY OF US CAN MAKE ABOUT THE ULTIMATE MYSTERIES OF LIFE IS SIMPLY RIDICULOUS.

. "God exists, and God is like this."

Or

"God doesn't exist."

Both pronouncements are made by us micro-micro sub-atomic specks clinging to a grain of sand planet swirling in an insignificant solar system in one of a couple of billion galaxies containing 1×10^{24} of stars in an expanding universe, all the while we can't even understand how a sea turtle gets back to lay her eggs on a tiny beach.

And we can make pronouncements about God, the very God who may have created that first galaxy and the latest iteration of sea turtle?

We say this from our slender, slender perspective on things. It's like an ant looking up at Mt. Everest and thinking, "Well, it's not *that* big."

If we're going to be honest with ourselves and escape from the delusions of our security-seeking mind, we must start with a strong dose of humility. We're simply not capable of being God-like, although we foolishly think we are.

A man named Paul in the New Testament expressed this brilliantly.

This prolific letter writer once pondered the human predicament. In doing so, he made this confession:

> We know that the Law is spiritual, but I'm made of flesh and blood…I don't know what I'm doing, because I don't do what I want to do. Instead, I do the thing that I hate. (Romans 7:14-15)

Even though he couched what he said in religious language, he could have just as easily expressed himself in secular terms: "I'm not in control of my life. At times I don't know why I say and do the things I say and do."

That's a pretty big admission. Before the advent of psychology, Paul had a fairly good handle on his limitations. Understanding his inability to be in control of his life, he took a leap of faith. Jesus is Lord, he proclaimed, and Christianity was born.

Maybe God is the answer for you in trying to gain some control over the uncontrollable.

Maybe something else is.

Regardless, without admitting our limitations, we will continue in the self-deception of being the narcissistic center of our self-created cosmos. That's fine if you're happy with the deception. People who pay good money to self-promoting televangelists are happy with their fantasy.

If you and I want to gain some authentic clarity as best we can, though, we must first admit that truth is a whack-a-mole type of thing. Just when we think we have it, something pops up and draws our attention away. We're incapable of having truth just pop up and stay there.

That's because we're not who we think we are.

That also means that God, if there is a God, isn't who we think God is.

Chapter Five—*God Isn't Who You Think God Is*

Here's a fun exercise.

Set aside any assumptions you have about the nature of God, if there is (or could be) a God. That is, you aren't from any faith tradition, nor have read any sacred texts.

Now pretend there is a God. Based solely on your observations of the world, your thoughts and experiences, answer the question,

Who Is God?
(write your reflections below)

What did you write?

"Someone who loves me."

"Someone who doesn't care."

"Someone who is too smart and too aloof."

"Someone who is a life force, a spirit living within all things."

Maybe your thoughts resembled those of people who described God on urbandictionary.com. According to them, the Almighty is:

The reason I passed math.

The main character in the fiction work "The Bible."

An entity whose opinions on the consumption of pork has been a matter of hot debate amongst the world's religions.

A voice that talks to you from the announcement speaker, "Cleanup in aisle 3!"

Man's most deadly creation.

A widely-known imaginary friend.

The reason for anything currently unexplained or unknown.

Such a hodge-podge of divine descriptions isn't surprising, given our immense limitations as homo sapiens. Whatever image we come up with regarding God, it says more about us than about God.

Michael Singer, in his book *The Untethered Soul*, states this very well. He notes that the world is filled with a variety of teachings, concepts and views about the deity. There are also many books considered sacred because they have words attributed to God. Yet all these revered thoughts have been touched by people. The one thing they have in common is that they seem to reflect the culture in which they were conceived.

When you combine human fallibility with human need, you can bank on the fact that no one living on this planet can be objectively sure of whom God is, if there is a God. Every statement about God that a person makes is incomplete because we're incomplete. We'll have competing, chaotic views.

To admit this is, I think, is healthy. When you believe you have God in your pocket, especially when it's profitable for you, you are not a fun person to be around. But when you make your statements about God and at the same time have the grace to say, "But I could be wrong," then you may be getting somewhere.

This is actually a very Biblical thing to do.

There are three curious places in the Bible that reflect this.

One is a phrase that is sprinkled throughout the pages almost sixty times:

"Fear of the Lord."

That can be taken a few ways, one of which is negative.

To Christians it seems harsh. If God is love and all that, why should you fear such a parent-like deity? You're supposed to feel warm and cuddly, like you would sitting on grandma's lap. To be afraid of God? That's so Old Testament.

There is, though, something very real and honest about that phrase.

For all the intimacy we Christians claim we have with God, we should admit that such a grandparental-like view can't mask the fact that God is God and not us. God can't fit neatly into our world view.

We have no idea why bad things happen to good people, if God is good. We don't know for sure when that diagnosis is going to come that begins with "stage four..." You could be gone before you end this chapter and before you could cruise over to friendlyatheist.org.

In other words, there's a lot of capriciousness out there. It shakes our security blanket. Sure, God can be love. Sure, a grizzly bear can be friendly. But in the end, neither God nor bear is us. God, if there is a God, should make us at the very least a little nervous.

Truly, in the words of a Hebrew songwriter, "The fear of the LORD is the beginning of wisdom; all those who practice it have a good understanding" (Psalm 111:10).

The second instance of the indescribability of the Almighty is in an interesting story buried in the Book of Exodus.

Moses has been following God's orders and has led the Hebrews out of slavery in Egypt. He's tired of simply hearing a voice. He wants to see the One who interrupted his career as a shepherd and turned him into a revolutionary:

> Moses said, "Please show me your glorious presence."
> The LORD said, "I'll make all my goodness pass in front of you, and I'll proclaim before you the name, 'The LORD.' I will be kind to whomever I wish to be kind, and I will have compassion to whomever I wish to be compassionate. But," the LORD said, "you can't see my face because no one can see me and live."
> The LORD said, "Here is a place near me where you will stand beside the rock. As my glorious presence passes by, I'll set you in a gap in the rock, and I'll cover you with my hand until I've passed by. Then I'll take away my hand, and you will see my back, but my face won't be visible." (Exodus 33:18-23)

This tale sounds ancient, which of course it is. Yet it is so spot on with our reflecting about God. We microscopic specks called human cannot understand the ways of the Creator of this ever-expanding universe. "See" God face to face? It's like looking directly at the sun without an eclipse viewer filter. There has to be something between you and the blazing thermonuclear reactor or you'll get fried.

It's rather refreshing to read such a bold, right to the point story in the Bible.

The third place where God's otherness is on full display is in the Book of Job. Actually, the whole book is a testimony to not getting too comfortable with the LORD.

Job suffers, legendarily. His three friends "console" him by saying that he's brought his suffering on because he's sinned, since it's common knowledge that God punishes sinners and rewards good people (like the three friends).

Job protests, letting God have it in the process. He's always been meticulous in avoiding sin, so God must be unjust in letting this happen. God's a corrupt judge, a big bully and a murderer. Such blasphemy drives his buddies into a feeding frenzy of protecting the LORD'S honor.

The twist at the end of the book is that God praises Job for his honesty and lays low his friends. God tells one of the guys, "I'm angry at you and your two friends because you haven't spoken about me correctly as did my servant Job" (Job 42:7).

The conventional wisdom about God is turned upside down. If God blesses a blasphemer and blasts the men toeing the party line about the divine, then what in the world are you supposed to think about such a deity?

Exactly the point.

The Bible is amazingly refreshing in places in resonating with our honest questions.

However, as we've already seen, there are a few other portraits of God painted in its pages that can be conflicting and confusing.

Just as God isn't who you think God is, neither is the Bible.

Chapter Six—*The Bible Isn't What You Think It Is*

When you start talking about God, at least from a Judeo-Christian perspective, you usually end up referencing the Bible in some way.

This doesn't prove anything to anyone other than to fellow believers, of course. To non-believers, the Bible isn't necessarily a good tool for faith. Actually, it could be a roadblock. Below are some of their objections.

NO "WORD" PROCESSING

It's common to take the Bible off the shelf and treat it as if the authors who penned the material used word processors, complete with spelling and grammar checkers. We expect it to be laid out logically. We expect it to make sense and be consistent.

This is what we'd want from any book, so why not from the most popular one of all time?

Unfortunately, the Bible was not born in the sterile birthing room of a publishing house, with authors who submitted their honed material electronically. It did not descend from on high, pristine and clear. Nor did God exert divine control over the writer's hand.

The substance of the Bible, instead, was given birth in a very messy way.

It started in story form, passed down from generation to generation. The tales were told with the passion of people seeking security, consistency and identity. They were also told within a culture that had no concept of modern science. It was believed that the earth was flat, that the sky was a metallic dome that shielded us from the waters of chaos, and that there was a mysterious underworld called Sheol. Everything was magical and mystical, and anything could happen, which is why you have those really weird tales.

Eventually the stories and teachings came to be written down. They were penned over a span of about 1,000 years. A lot changed during that millennium. There were the rise and fall of nations. There was a civil war in Israel. The Assyrians, Babylonians, Persians, Greeks and Romans all conquered the Hebrews. Their views of the world, and their gods with their stories, became known. Hence, concepts change. You go from Sheol in the Old Testament being a nice resting place for the dead to hell in the New Testament, where the last thing you get is rest.

Finally, the Hebrew books were collected and became the Hebrew Scriptures, popularly called the Old Testament. The Christian books ultimately were collected and became what we call the New Testament. In the process, some Hebrew and Christian books didn't make the sacred cut, so they became a secondary source of inspiration called the "Apocrypha."

Such is the unkempt genesis of the Bible you hold in your hands or view online today.

BARBARIC VIEWS

Another problem people have with the Bible is that there are things in it that are an affront to our modern sensibilities. Here's a partial list:

Killing every living thing in towns defeated by Israel.
Killing rebellious children.
Killing homosexuals.
Torturing people in hell.
Offering your daughters to be raped.
Punishing future generations for the sins of ancestors.

Critics wonder how people who believe the Bible to be literally infallible accept this without thinking, ascribing God to be behind some of these things. The need for security and identity trumps the insecurity that may come from rational reflection.

WILD TALES

Coinciding with barbarisms are stories that sound like fairy tales:
Eve being formed from a rib then talking to a snake.
Male angels mating with female humans to form a race of giants.
A woman being turned into salt because she was curious.
Jonah living inside a hungry whale.
A Jewish Captain Israel (Samson) killing a thousand enemies with a donkey's jawbone.
An angry prophet (Elisha) cursing teens who made fun of his baldness, resulting in bears attacking them.
Walking around in a furnace.
The sun standing still.

This list only scratches the surface, and it makes some scratch their heads.

In ancient times, when magic and flat earth-center-of-the-universe reigned, some of these tales could make sense. But in the age of Hawking, quantum mechanics and string theory, they're a stretch.

Certainly stories that make us scratch our heads may nonetheless carry meaning for us today. Some spawn lessons and sermons. Yet it's easy to lose that meaning when we're more concerned about whether or not they happened. If they didn't objectively happen, does that diminish their significance, or the truth of the Bible?

LANGUAGE PROBLEMS

The problem with the Bible to modern ears isn't only that it contains barbarisms and outlandish tales. There's also the problem that we don't understand what it really says in places.

These sacred books were written originally in different languages, as kingdoms rose and fell. Hebrew, Aramaic and Greek. They were then translated into other languages, and sometimes the intent conveyed in the original words was difficult to translate. What's more, over time the earliest material on which the books were written became corrupt; writing on papyrus isn't exactly like storing something in the cloud. Thus, some of the letters in the original language became unreadable. There could also be two manuscripts for a section of a book, and one has an addition that the other doesn't. This is why you have footnotes on some passages saying, "Hebrew uncertain" or "other manuscripts say..."

Just because we see the words in our native tongue doesn't mean those are the original ones.

Take once again my favorite book, Job. That's the writing with the most "Hebrew uncertain" disclaimers. Such footnotes are meaning, "Here's our best guess as to what this word means; good luck."

A good example is the different translations of Job 38:36.

Here's the New Revised Standard's:
   Who has put wisdom in the inward parts,
or given understanding to the mind?

Here is the Common English rendering:
   Who put wisdom in remote places,
or who gave understanding to a rooster?

The Message translates it:

Who do you think gave weather-wisdom to the ibis,
and storm-savvy to the rooster?

And finally, the Amplified version has:
Who has put wisdom in the innermost being [of man, or in the layers of clouds]
Or given understanding to the mind [of man, or to the heavenly display]?

So, according to what you read, the verse contains anything from heart and mind to roosters, clouds and ibises.

Illustrations like this should serve as a solid warning to anyone who claims that paper Pope status for the Bible. If you can't be certain what it says, how infallible is that Pope?

BOTH INCONSISTENCIES AND INCONSISTENT USE

It's easy to assume that if the Bible were the perfect, literally inerrant Word of God, then there should be no inconsistencies. It should flow seamlessly and coherently from Genesis to Revelation.

That's our bias, though, and not that of the ancient writers.

As the early books of the Bible formed, various stories were compiled within them without a regard for uniformity. You don't have a pepperoni pizza when it comes to sacred scripture. You have a supreme, sporting a variety of toppings scattered all over the place, some of which conflict (anchovy and pineapple?).

Here are some of the mixed ingredients:

Two different creation stories.

Multiple accounts of the Resurrection.

Conflicting records of events, such as God praising the establishment of kingship in Israel at one place and condemning it as faithlessness in another.

Conflicting views of God, from being a softie to a terminator; from being patient and easy going to you'd better not cross me or you'll be sorry; from being one who seeks out a lost sheep to one who barbeques that sheep if it doesn't return to the fold.

Some of the biggest inconsistencies center on conflicting teachings.

You have lots of prohibitions scattered throughout the Bible, especially in Leviticus (the anti-Job book). Yet you also have teachings that counter some of those restrictions.

As noted earlier, there are passages condemning homosexuality, supporting slavery and urging women to keep quiet. You also have teachings on the qualities of love in a committed relationship, on equality, and on freedom. These may run counter to each other.

The negatives and the positives seem to be in conflict, reflective of the ways people use the Scriptures are in conflict. Some focus on the Thou Shalt Nots, while others focus on the Why Nots.

It feels a bit uneasy writing the preceding, describing how the Bible appears to the outside world.

I've lived on the inside with the Bible since I was 15. It's connected me to God. I love it. I am thankful for the people who wrote it, cared for it, sacrificed for it, studied it and taught it. I've taken classes on it, written a commentary and curriculum about it, preached from it, led studies in it. I remain intrigued by it, perhaps because it is so messy, unorganized and inconsistent, like life that I'm discovering now that I'm in my 60's.

Maybe the greatest praise of the Bible is that it is a wonderful companion through every stage of life. In every phase, there's something in it that's amazingly, mysteriously relevant. I believe that's a reflection of God present in those pages.

However, like life itself, the one thing the Bible will not do is chart a clear path for undeniable, undoubt-able, faith. You can't just pick it up and find God. If you try, you'll only find what you want to find and disregard the rest.

Scripture speaks to both saint and sinner. It's just that it has to be approached in an open, vulnerable way.

There's work we have to do if we're serious about ever developing a faith that makes sense and feels right.

We've accomplished the first part of that task, the deconstructing phase.

It's time now to turn the corner.

<u>Turning</u>

God is not found in the soul by adding anything, but by a process of subtraction.

--Meister Eckhart

Chapter Seven—*Honesty and Humility, In That Order*

Here's a quick recap of what we've covered up to this point.

Humans are dynamic creatures with genetic predispositions and a subconscious drive for security, consistency and identity. We have ever-changing brains that will think differently at 20 than at 50 or 80. Meanwhile, we're infinitesimal particles clinging to a grain of sand planet whirling in an insignificant solar system floating in an ever-expanding universe populated by trillions of stars and solar systems. Also, sea turtles baffle us.

The people who wrote the Bible are like this. The people who were great theologians are like this. The people who are raging or friendly atheists are like this. The people who hawk donations on TV or ring the Salvation Army bell at Christmas are like this.

Scratch the surface and we're all united in our limitations and subjectivity. None of us knows the truth with a capitol T.

There's no escaping this destiny.

We can either continue living in the fantasy world that we have it all together and, gee, wouldn't it be great if everyone saw things like I see them? Or we can claim our basic, united humanity and endeavor to nurture a couple of virtues that can go a long way in opening us to an absolutely amazing world, regardless of the labels with which we tag ourselves.

HONESTY

Honesty is admitting that you'll never be able to figure things out with certainty and that perhaps some of the answers you think you've come up with may not earn you an A.

There is something refreshing and releasing about this.

Remember how our brain overheats in writing those creative stories helping you make sense of things, Quaaluding you with the fantasy of security?

What if you recognized the myths, preconceptions and prejudices you hold that fuel those stories? What if you let them go and approach living with total openness?

For believer and non-believer alike, such honesty produces a different texture for life. Relaxed from your preoccupation of making sense of things, the world becomes a bit more interesting and colorful.

Remember "confirmation bias" in law enforcement, when you look only for those things that prove what you want to prove? Removing your need to bend life to your bias means that you see things from a much broader perspective. When you don't have to confirm anything, the horizon grows wider.

Another example from law enforcement is the interrogation technique of asking a suspect to continually repeat their story. If they're lying, they will invariably trip up on a detail and contradict themselves. It takes a lot of energy to keep together a narrative you've made up or want to believe.

Being honest with ourselves, on the other hand, gives us energy for what's important. Relinquishing the neurotic belief that we stand on the cornerstone of truth might make our journey in this life a lot cleaner, if not clearer. If you can't at least temporarily suspend your belief or non-belief system in the name of honesty, you'll always spend useless energy in storytelling-to-self mode. You'll limit the people you talk with to the ones who share bits of your story. You'll actually believe the Facebook algorithms that feed you only news that supports your political/religious/social perspective on things, giving you the hallucination that you and your kind have it all together.

How refreshing to give up that burden. How humanizing instead of de-humanizing.

Ultimately, dropping our pretenses (or "repenting" if you prefer) leads us to an approach to life that counters the clamoring of modern legalists:

HUMILITY

Honesty is a passive thing. It says I'm going to drop my delusions and live as openly as I can.

Humility is an active thing. It drives me to cultivate a lifestyle that really affirms I don't know everything, and that that's all right. In my thinking, feeling, acting and talking, I'm going to be a rookie.

Paul in the New Testament, whom we saw earlier in Chapter 4, admitted being out of control in his life. That's honesty. He then turned that into the virtue of humility.

In addressing an eating problem in one of his churches, he summarized his solution this way:

> The question keeps coming up regarding meat that has been offered up to an idol: Should you attend meals where such meat

is served, or not? We sometimes tend to think we know all we need to know to answer these kinds of questions but sometimes our humble hearts can help us more than our proud minds. We never really know enough until we recognize that God alone knows it all. (1 Corinthians 8:1-3, The Message)

"Our humble hearts can help us more than our proud minds."

That means we might not necessarily know the solution to a problem, or if there are multiple solutions, or even if there is a solution.

That means other people can teach us a thing or two if we seek them out and listen.

That means that there may be things in this world that will present new insights if we don't force the issue but simply be open to receiving them.

That means that we can teach, preach, believe what we want, but if we're honest and humble, we'll always teach, preach and believe with the caveat, *But there could be more to the story*. As a wise priest once prayed, "I try to do your will, Lord, but just because I think it's your will doesn't necessarily mean that it is."

We can learn a lot if we believe we have a lot left to learn.

Reviewing the above thoughts, it's striking how simplistic and naïve it all sounds.

Admit that I don't have a corner on the truth? Admit that people with differing views might be my teacher?

Right.

Every cell in our brains fights against this. We might stand a better chance at changing our ingrained personalities.

The higher, critical thinking part of our internal computer could reason, "'Honesty and humility.' That sounds sensible."

Our base brain has another idea.

"No! Are you out of your mind?"

To REALLY be honest and humble would make us vulnerable. Our self-driving, storytelling sub-conscious will have none of that.

Every door we may try to open for true dialogue with someone will, at least at first, seem stuck. Our mental baggage is leaning against it on the other side, resisting our efforts.

Likewise, whenever we ask a risky, open-ended question, we'll have an internal nudge to settle quickly for a simplistic, generalized answer that's in line with our bias. We don't really want to hear what those dragons lurking in uncharted waters might teach us. It's safe to pretend that either they don't exist or, if they do, they're like the Wizard of Oz, all bluster and no substance.

Maybe the opposite of honesty and humility isn't deceit and arrogance. It's just plain fear. Fear that maybe our internal story isn't totally correct, after all. Fear that our understanding of life might have a large dose of misunderstanding mixed in.

Fear promotes the rabid us-them mentality that infests our society. It's why America is the most divided we've ever been since the Civil War. We're all afraid, so we seek tribal security by retreating behind political lines. Everything is a lot more consistent when we live within such a limited perspective of the truth. The whole truth is frightening, requiring honesty and humility to see its breadth. A party-line truth is much more manageable.

I'd like to think (again, naïvely) that our shared quest for meaning in life can bring about a fragment of healing to some of our society's gaping wounds.

Whereas we'll never agree politically, we can agree that the world is a huge, mysterious place full of awe, wonder and danger. Hopefully we can agree we need one another to help us find our path through it.

Honesty and humility are the only way we can bridge our differences and move ahead.

Having preached this preceding two-point sermon, I must confess these are not easily assumable virtues for me.

I am a Christian. I've been that way for almost 50 years. I don't see myself changing. Yet the security I get from my belief system is a leash that restrains me from being totally open to considering other views, some of which may differ from my own. It's like a law of spiritual inertia. "A person who feels secure in their beliefs will remain at rest."

I would assume an atheist would feel the same way, if they're totally candid.

Questioning and admitting limitations shouldn't be seen as a weakness. Rather, it should be more a sign of character strength.

Honesty and humility make us real with whom we uniquely are in life. Dependency, openness and vulnerability are not four-letter words. As we strive to make them part of our internal vocabulary, we may begin to change a bit.

As we change, the world we see will change.

Chapter Eight—*Transcendence and Gratitude*

Thirty years ago I took a group of college students to Colorado for a ski trip. I was a campus minister at the University of Missouri at the time and thought such a trip would be a wonderful way of combining work and fun.

Early on the morning we were to return, I drove the van down the heaven known as Winter Park. I later wrote these words to describe the experience:

> The sun had just risen and was hanging lazily over the horizon.
>
> Around every turn on that twisty, narrow Berthoud Pass road awaited a new, breath-taking scene. Snow-capped peaks silhouetted against a deep blue sky, with blasts of frigid wind creating sparkling snow clouds at the summit. Or birch, evergreens and aspens standing as a family on a mountainside, with the sun delicately etching their shadows on a blanket of brilliant-white snow. Or cascading valleys so steep and deep you couldn't even see the bottom; you could only see trees and snow disappearing into shadowy ravines.
>
> As the van crept along timidly, an eerie sensation engulfed me. The startling beauty of that mountainous world was coming home. As one panorama gave way to another, I began feeling as if I were on foreign, but not alien, soil. I felt as if I were driving through God's estate, and that at any moment, around any curve, I could come face to face with the Almighty. I felt very close to the Creator. The divine breath blew against my cheek and the thunder of God's heartbeat rang in my ears.

This might sound overly poetic, yet that's what happens when you have a transcendent experience. You lose the language of the left-brain.

The definition of transcendence should be this: What you feel when your left-brain (analytical) takes a break, freeing the right-brain (creative) to escape and play.

When the right brain plays, then things appear differently. You're not concerned about yesterday or tomorrow; there's only now, right now. You're not concerned about making sense of things but feeling connected to things. You're not racing but you're pacing, slowing down to discover shades, textures, vibrancy.

What do you call the world you encounter thusly, not to manipulate and understand but to enjoy and feel?

Some will call it the experience of God.

This is central to Rabbi Jamie S. Korngold's theology. Not surprisingly, she bases her ministry, the "Adventure Rabbi" program, in the mountains of the Western United States. In her book, *The God Upgrade*, she notes other types of experiences in nature that can trigger this feeling, such as sunsets, meteor showers and a walk by a lake. When she's led people in nature excursions, she's impressed by how they sense a closeness with each other. They share the feeling of insignificance in the vastness of creation.

It's not just in nature that such experiences occur, of course. The birth of a child. A piece of music. A turn of phrase. And suddenly life takes on a depth and breadth that you'd missed when you were busy paying the bills.

Sometimes it just happens in the ordinary.

Marcus Borg related transcendent experiences he had had throughout his lifetime. The first was when he was in his thirties, while driving through a winter landscape in Minnesota. Those moments would randomly appear for the next couple of years. Then nothing until he was in his fifties, during a flight.

The common factor in all this for him was that the light changed to "yellowy and golden." Everything was bathed in this light. He was amazed at how beautiful the world became, including some ugly guy on a plane from Tel Aviv who now appeared "wondrous." Borg also related a feeling of connectedness, like Rabbi Korngold described. In the yellowy-golden light, the subject-object relationship fell away; he sensed a union with his surroundings, including strangers. He stated later that he wished he could have lived with this heightened consciousness forever. The best word he came up with to describe such a world was "glorious." (*Convictions*)

Father Richard Rohr, a Franciscan friar, calls this the experience of "wonder." In his book, *The Naked Now*, he talks about different eyes through which we see. We can look at life simplistically, enjoying it without asking too many questions. We can look at life rationally, seeking to understand. Or we can look at life holistically, sensing the beauty, seeking answers, but ultimately looking at the larger picture of life and connecting the dots.

Transcendent moments are those times we see through what he calls the "third eye." It's something that happens when our heart, mind and body are totally open and receptive to the fullness of a moment. This is what he means by the "naked" experience. You can experience full joy or full sorrow. Regardless, you are transported out of your rigid, analytical outlook and allowed to be vulnerable to what life has for you in that moment.

Journalist Michael Pollan wrote *How to Change Your Mind*, detailing his trip down the transcendent lane by exploring psychedelic drugs. He had described himself as ascribing to a "materialist philosophy," where matter is all that mattered, and things could be understood by physical laws.

Then in his research he grew amazed at the effects of drugs that affected the way we see ordinary things. Pharmaceuticals such as LSD had the effect of suppressing the mind's constant chatter and activity. Suddenly a whole new reality opened up. As in the experiences noted above, what was happening today, in vivid detail, became important. It was indescribable. Even a leaf would take on luminescent beauty. Such a broader way of experiencing things could produce a "crack" in the narrow materialistic mindset.

There is nothing unique about the above people. Anyone can suddenly feel as if they're no longer in Kansas but rather in some strange and wonderful Land of Oz.

William James documents this in his classic, *The Varieties of Religious Experience*. He says such experiences are simply part of being human, no matter who you are. He also does not claim that their source is necessarily God. Rather, he simply documents the diverse ways people's ordinary lives can suddenly, without warning, be shot through with expanded perception. We are creatures with the physical capability of transcending limiting mindsets. Our brains are simply wired to expand consciousness and awareness.

It would be a shame to downplay the transcendent experiences we have because they can't be measured or understood. They point to a perceived reality that is felt to be just as "real" as that of the empirical world of science. Some people who have had them, including scientists, have had their outlook on life permanently altered and can never again live comfortably solely with test tubes and theories.

Some may believe such experiences prove the reality of a spiritual world and of God's existence. Others will say that they are just a part of our biological makeup.

I think they point to the limitations of both exclusive rationalism and emotionally-needy faith. Transcendent experiences prick the balloon we blow up with our warm air, thinking we can understand life's many layers. Transcendence also shows that those moments are universal and not bound to born-again Christians; they are remarkably egalitarian and beyond formula or creed.

For all who are honest and humble, they are a wonderful sign that we are not in control in this world. At any moment our nice, contained, predictable surroundings might be thrown topsy-turvy. For all the fright that engenders, there's also unexpected beauty and indescribable joy.

That's something for which to be grateful.

Here's a thought that adds to that gratefulness.

An article appearing on the phys.org website detailed a study done regarding the Fermi Paradox. This is a physics problem that posed the question, "If there is so much life in the universe, where is everybody?"

A group of scientists crunched the numbers and arrived at the conclusion that we are likely the only advanced civilization in the observable universe. In other words, we are all alone out there. It's just us, on this celestial crumb.

If this is true, think of how special that makes life on earth.

Even though we are those microscopic specks on a grain of sand planet, how astounding it is that everything has coalesced to the point that we can live, and be at least semi-intelligent in so doing.

Astrophysicist Paul Wallace, in his book *Stars Beneath Us*, writes that for life to have happened here, a lot of things had to have occurred just right. He says it's like standing fifteen feet from a wall. On the wall are scattered six small squares that are each a half-inch on a side. You are given six darts and then blindfolded. You then are told to throw all six darts in one heave. You do so, remove the blindfold, and see that all of them have hit their tiny targets.

The likelihood of the darts doing that is the likelihood that there could be life on our planet. I like to think it points to God the Creator's doing. Others will say it's blind chance. What ultimately matters is that, against such astronomical odds, we have life, and it is astoundingly good.

Yes, gratitude is in order.

Every breath, every heartbeat, every blink, every note, every color. All a gift.

Add to that a life that's shot through with moments that are yellowy-golden, and thankfulness is the outcome.

It's in such moments of transcendent gratitude that we see all our arguments being what they are. Petty. Our struggles with each other reflect un-gratitude. We live in a huge ice cream store and we fight over which flavor of vanilla we want, French or Classic. Our sniping over so many issues, including God, reflects a refusal to see the whole assortment of flavors right in front of us.

Transcendent moments that result in a grateful outlook on life do wondrous things.

If we take them seriously, then we will get along with each other better. Things that tick us off won't seem so tick-able.

What's more, if we allow for the transcendent in our lives, then perhaps a new door could begin creaking open a bit.

What it reveals is a strange world.

Chapter Nine—*Mystery: A Collection of Strange Events*

NOTE: What you're about to read is going to cross the line for some. If you don't want to cross that line because you feel it's transgressing intellectual boundaries as you begin reading, feel free to skip to the next chapter. Truly, I mean that. You can pick right up where we ended with the preceding one. That's preferable to dismissing our time together at this point with, "Well, he's lost it." If you read the following without pre-judging, however, it may add some depth and color to the rest of this book.

Transcendence, with the resulting attitude of gratitude, opens life up to us. It's like popping a cork on a merlot and pouring a glass. You don't just start sipping. You let it sit there and breathe. Oxygen deepens the flavor.

Things happen that interrupt everyday-ness and make you reconsider things. Mixing metaphors, such things are like earthquakes. Some are a mild tremor, and you carry on after the initial movement subsides. Others rock the Richter scale, and you have to deal with the cracks that have formed in your foundation.

The tales below are personal experiences when my Richter needle pegged out.

THE CROSS INCIDENT

As referenced before, I'd had one of those deeply moving religious experiences at age 15.

As months passed, the thought of pursuing the ordained ministry popped into my head. I had some qualms about this. After all, it is your life choice. Additionally, being an adolescent, it was an all or nothing, life or death, matter.

Having rural ties, I was out in a field clearing underbrush one day. That meant noisy hours with a chainsaw. That also meant, based on such an experience, that the last thing on my choice-of-desirable-jobs list was farming.

While going about this delightful pursuit, I paused to take a break. Laying down the chainsaw, an odd shape seemed to jump out at me.

It was a cross formed by two sticks. They had grown together at almost perfect 90-degree angles. The only thing out of proportion was the left horizontal section, which was a little long. Also strange was the vertical stick. It wasn't straight but curved in the crucifix shape of what you usually associate with the body of Jesus hanging on the cross.

What do you make of this?

I took it as a sign, of course. I was looking for some direction and saw what I wanted/needed to see.

On the other hand, what's the big deal? Such a coincidence of finding those sticks at that particular time is nothing more than randomness in action. Some people find four-leaf clovers. This just happens to be a little more bizarre.

Yet, why would we want to dismiss something we can't explain? To quickly discount the mysterious may reflect our uneasiness with the mysterious. Perhaps the more honest and humble approach is to grant at least the possibility that there could be things operating beyond our rational faculties.

That natural sculpture has found a home in every pastor's office I've occupied. Its weirdness lingers. There may be a rational explanation of how two sticks could grow together on their own in crucifix proportion, then end up at the exact place I put down the chainsaw during a time when I was trying to figure out my life's calling.

But how will you know for sure?

Maybe that's how you define, and live with, mystery.

DAD'S DEATH

My father lay dying.

He'd celebrated his 90th birthday just two days before. He'd enjoyed himself at the party thrown for him at his assisted living home. He'd had birthday cake and asked for a beer to go with it, which proves that when you're 90, you can and should order anything you want. He thoroughly enjoyed himself, while the rest of us tried not to think of the odd combination.

The next day he slipped into a coma. (I don't think it had anything to do with the blend of chocolate cake and Budweiser.) It was now only a matter of time, but how much?

I've been around dying people enough to know that death is never, *never*, on cue. You can't schedule the day, hour, minute, second of your demise. Our mortality clutches the illusion of immortality to the very end, and not a microsecond before. It's only in Hollywood that the body gives up that easily and quickly, so as not to belabor the plot.

Dad's body was on automatic. His mouth had dropped open and rhythmically, as if it were a human respirator, his chest sucked in air, held it for a count, then released.

Mid-afternoon I knelt by his bed, held his calloused farmer's hand, and silently offered up a prayer. Actually, it wasn't as much a prayer to God as it was to Dad. I addressed him, "You can go. I love you, but I can go on now without you."

I continued this monologue in my mind, watching him as I did. And before I finished, he simply exhaled one breath and didn't take another. He died, just as I was telling him it was OK to die. He didn't die before I prayed or after I prayed, but while I prayed. Witnessing this, I discovered that when someone says, "The hair on the back of my neck stood up," you should believe that person. That's what happened to me, watching Dad leave us. Time seemed frozen. Along with raised neck hair were goose bumps.

Did he have the power consciously to choose to die at that moment?

Did he hear me in a way that didn't require ears?

Did he also hear or see others inviting him to come on over?

There are no answers that will satisfy the Hawking in us. I only know that Dad's death was a transcendent coincidence that made me firmly believe that there are different levels of perception other than that caused by the chemical firing of neurons.

A lot of study has been done on Near Death Experiences. Some talk about them being a chemical thing (Dr. Kevin Nelson, *The Spiritual Doorway in the Brain*), while others (Dr. Eben Alexander, *Heaven Is Real*) present evidence that we have a consciousness separate from the cranial cortex. While I can't talk about NDEs, I can talk about my Dad's DE. You simply don't die on cue, unless something else beyond our understanding is going on.

And therein lies the intersection between rationality and mystery.

"Something else beyond our understanding is going on."

THE TRANSMISSION HESITATION

Of the many things that change when you have children, your driving habits are the most obvious.

When you have a scrap of humanity in a car seat in the back, you make sure seatbelts are fastened, the speed limit is observed, and you look both ways, several times.

My wife and I were stopped at a light. I was driving, Barbara was in the passenger seat and behind her, safely nestled in his car seat, was our six-month-old son, Cameron.

The light turned green and I stepped on the accelerator. The engine revved, but we didn't move.

Looking down, I discovered that the gearshift was in neutral.

"That's strange," I said to Barb, as we glanced at each other.

Shifting it into drive, we eased out into the intersection when …WHOOSH … a tow truck, barreling down from the right, runs the light and barely misses our bumper. We would have been in the middle of the intersection had there not been that transmission hesitation. The truck would have caught us broadside.

I don't know how the car shifted into neutral. Obviously I did it, but I don't remember doing it or why I would have done it in the first place. It just happened. There is no doubt that it saved the lives of my wife and child.

Why did it happen? And why are there other occasions where Maximas venture into intersections on time, without any mysterious delay, and get t-boned by a Mack truck? And why might I get broadsided by a bus when I pull out of this parking lot, distracted by my bagel?

I don't know. I can only be grateful for a transmission that slipped into neutral at that particular time.

THE BIG BLACK DOG

My wife and I encountered a most unusal dog on a cold December day, 2010.

That year had been one of transition. We had moved, transplanting our family, and I had begun ministry in a new church. With all the excitement of going to a wonderful new parish with great people, there were also anxieties and concerns. Uprooting mixes a strange cocktail of grieving goodbyes with hopeful hellos. It is difficult, especially when you have young children.

The family mood at Christmas was a bit melancholy, accordingly. The cold, gray Missouri surroundings certainly didn't lift one's spirits.

But somehow a dog did.

My wife and I had decided to take a walk on the day following the holiday. We were visiting her parents, who live across the state from us. We don't get back there more than once or twice a year.

There are dogs in the large, rural subdivision where my in-laws live. They don't usually bother you. There's an unwritten (of course) country canine code that says you can bark but can't leave your own yard. Such is the way of non-urban dogs.

However, on this walk, after going about a mile and a half, a big black lab sauntered up behind us, wagging his tail. We stopped and petted it. It then did the most unusual thing.

This incredibly friendly dog walked on ahead, as if leading us. We came to a "T" in the road, and the dog turned left: just the direction we would turn. Eventually there was another "T," and he turned left: again, the direction we were going. After a while, a road intersected from the right. Instead of continuing ahead, he turned right: once again, our direction.

This was getting eerie.

He stayed on that road a bit until he veered off into the front yard of my in-laws' house. He sat down and waited for us to go inside. Once inside, I looked out and saw him returning whence he came.

We'd never seen the dog before. He didn't know us, we didn't know him. Yet he led us, like an old friend, to the house.

There was something comforting about this. It was like the dog was conveying a sense of, "It's OK. You all are not alone. You have guidance and companionship."

Granted, my brain was really working on a doozy of a story here. Nonetheless, it was a sense both my wife and I felt.

Ever the pessimist, I decided to walk the same route the next day. At the identical point, the lab trotted out to meet me. This time, instead of leading, he followed. After a short distance he stopped, scratched, then turned up the road in the opposite direction, oblivious to me.

Whatever had possessed the dog the day before was gone.

Sure, "whatever." A weird coincidence. Who can decipher the complexities (or lack thereof) of a canine brain? But when was the last time a dog you'd never seen before, while you're visiting from out of town, leads you home?

Such are four of my strange events. If you've taken intellectual offense at them, remember that you were warned in the beginning.

Absolutely, you can dismiss them as wishful thinking on my part. It's reading meaning into things that just occur, like seeing shapes in clouds or Elvis in a blob of jelly. Neanderthals and homo sapiens have been doing this since their cave dwelling days.

Indeed, my interpretations of the preceding tales could stem from my wanting confirmation that there is a mysterious Force that's with me, working behind the scenes at just the right time. I want to let that storytelling part of my brain have good material with which to work.

I fully admit and confess this limitation. In my intellectual bias, which is a way of trying to stay in control, I can dismiss them. I can join the long list of skeptics who would do this, for the sake of intellectual honesty.

Yet, also for intellectual honesty's sake, I can't set them aside without having a nagging doubt about my doubt.

These things happened without my prompting, like Borg's yellowy-golden light thing. I'm left to deliberate, using the computing power of my clunky cerebral motherboard. I'm left with the possibility that there's a lot more to the world than we see on the surface. And if the world is a lot deeper than it appears, just how deep does it go?

It prods me to loosen up the forged chains of rationality.

At the same time, I can't make too much of such events. It's not appropriate to lose all boundaries and prop them up as objective miracles worthy of some candle-lit shrine. They shouldn't be ends in themselves. That's like those ghost-hunting TV shows where a paranormal investigator, upon the sound of a creaking board, calls out, "Did you hear that? DID YOU HEAR THAT?!" You'll always hear something if you're listening for it.

The bottom line is that, if you're honest with yourself and if you humbly realize you can't be the final judge on things, then there will be a healthy tension between the rational and the unknown. This adds intrigue to life.

I believe such events are simply gifts that come to anyone. Viewing them as calling cards from a deeper side of life, asking us to sit a while and let the wine continue to breathe and deepen before rushing to consume, is refreshing. It can affect how you read the Bible (if you do), pray (if you do) and relate to others.

I asked my congregation if they had tales of such strange things that have happened to them. Several submitted stories that make you pause and ponder. I've included some of them in Appendix A.

All such narratives point to a simple formula.

Transcendence plus gratitude opens mystery.
This leads us, finally, to Jesus.

Chapter Ten—*Jesus Isn't Who You Think He Is*

The problem with Jesus isn't Jesus.

It's with some of the people who rabidly believe in him as well as the ones who rabidly disbelieve.

Both can be tacky.

Google "memes of Jesus" and you get all sorts of stereotypical stuff. Usually they depict him as overly sweet or overly stern. Either way, he's become the butt of a lot of jokes.

Unbelievers with an attitude can be downright snarky. Here's an example, lifted from the net.

> CHRISTIANITY:
>
> The belief that some cosmic Jewish Zombie can make you live forever if you symbolically eat his flesh and telepathically tell him that you accept him as your master, so he can remove an evil force from your soul that is present in humanity because a rib-woman was convinced by a talking snake to eat from a magical tree.
>
> Makes perfect sense.

Jesus has become the litmus test of where you are in your outlook on things. He's Superman if you're a believer. He never existed, or he's a nice guy who's been hijacked by fundamentalists, if you're a non-believer.

There's not a lot of honesty and humility in either caricature. Remember, don't diddle with what gives someone security, be you saint or sinner.

Given the backdrop of this book, though, we're doing ourselves a disservice if we don't seriously consider him. If the world isn't imprisoned by the bars of either uncompromising rationality or fundamentalism, then Jesus can take on a different character.

He may become a key player in the transcendence plus gratitude produces mystery game.

To see his importance, let's start by relieving him of the religiosity with which he's been encumbered. Let's get back to how people felt about him when they didn't see him as a pleasant chap with soft eyes wearing a little halo.

Cruise through the Gospels and imagine how plain folk would have experienced him.

(There will be some disagreement about what the historical Jesus said and what early Christians said he said. This started a couple of hundred years ago with the "quest for the historical Jesus." If you'd like to go down that rabbit hole as a side excursion, you're welcomed to turn to Appendix B.)

Who is Jesus, in a general sense, according to the only sources we have of his life?

He is first and foremost a teacher.

Matthew records in his Gospel that after Jesus gave his first big message, the Sermon on the Mount, "the crowds were *astounded* at his teaching, for he taught them as one having *authority*." (Matthew 7:28-29)

Astonishment. Authority.

Get a load of the high points:

- He told his first listeners to love their enemies and do good to those who hate them.
- He told them that the God of the universe knew each of them intimately and sees and listens to them regularly.
- He told them if they're going to pray, pray in a closet where no one can see them and pray that God's will, not theirs, is done first.
- He told them that sin starts from the inside. A bad spirit gives rise to bad things.
- He told them not to worry so much. Trust that the God who had their hair number also had their back.
- He told them not to be quick to judge others but cut them some slack.
- He told them to treat others as you want to be treated.
- And to top all this off, he told them to be perfect as God is perfect.

I, too, would have been astounded, especially when the "eye for an eye, tooth for a tooth" thing was the norm of the day.

Probably his most mind-blowing words came in the context of his standing up to his enemies, who happened to be very powerful leaders of the religious/political establishment.

His most famous foes were the Pharisees. They were a sect within ancient Judaism that stressed cataloguing and keeping all 613 laws found in Hebrew scripture. These were the "thou shalts" and the "thou shalt nots." Pharisees knew them by heart, could recite them, and were quick to point out whenever anyone broke them...

...such as Jesus. He didn't transgress accidentally, either. He knew what he was doing.

Such a lawbreaker had to be confronted. You can't have anyone like that loose in society. His teachings about loving enemies and such would mess up everything. It's just like today. You can't have people trying to reconcile with each other. That's the one thing the far right and the far left agree on. There are those who are correct and then there's everyone else. You can't compromise. There must be winners and losers.

Jesus had to be stopped. His love/reconciliation thing would lead people into blasphemy/anarchy. Plus, the Pharisees would lose their power and status.

Their assault on Jesus started early in his ministry. It didn't take long for it to escalate. That's because he did what no one else had ever been able to do.

He put them in their place.

He intentionally threw gas on the fire of their anger and he didn't flinch from the heat. They exploded and threatened to kill him with that fire, but that didn't matter to him. He knew what he was talking about, he seemed to know Who he was talking about, and he was willing to accept the consequences.

As one of his enemies said in the rock opera *Jesus Christ Superstar*, "One thing I'll say for him, Jesus is cool!"

Look at how cool Jesus was in stoking the Pharisees' wrath.

- They made an adulterous woman stand with embarrassment in front of him. "The law says stone her, right?" They scowled as Jesus snared them in their hypocrisy. "OK, whichever one of you is a saint, here's a rock. You go first."
- They accused Jesus of working on the Sabbath when he healed the eyes of the blind and the legs of the lame. They scowled as he said that the broken, the outcast, the poor and the repentant sinner would get into heaven before holier-than-thou, self-righteous jerks.
- They tried to trick and trap him with questions about Jewish law. They scowled when he finally had enough and accused them of

being hypocrites, blind guides and white-washed tombs (pretty on the outside, but stinking and rotten on the inside).
- They called him an immoral drunk because he hung around "undesirables." They scowled as he said that, while their God was made in their own messed up image, his God resembled a heart-broken parent yearning for a wayward child, or a shepherd desperately searching for a strayed lamb.

Whew.

Too often people paint Jesus in shades of pastel, appearing as if he's on his way to a quilting party.

The real Jesus, though, mixed incredible compassion and crystal-clear insight with a grit of character that drove him to challenge the authorities without backing down an inch.

He dared do all this because he seemed to walk on a foundation that no one else could claim. There was an intimacy with the Jewish God that was strange and fairly blasphemous in his day.

You were supposed to not even utter God's name if you were a good Jew. The most you could do was mumble the Hebrew consonants YHWH, an unpronounceable word that's the source of "Jehovah." But what did Jesus call God? "Abba." Daddy. He would go off into the woods to talk with this unseen parent. He could sleep in a boat in the middle of a storm, confident that Dad would look after him. When he saw people desecrating the Temple by doing business in it and making a profit, he took it personally: "My *Father's* house is a house of prayer, but you have made it a den of thieves!"

It was ultimately this passion for God, and his trust in God, that led to his execution.

If there was ever a threat to the status quo, it was this Nazareth wild man.

He didn't die in his sleep. He was murdered because he had to be silenced. The religious and secular powers of his day saw to that.

What happened next is the make-or-break point of Christianity.

It's fitting that a man who lived as largely as Jesus lived had to have an amazing footnote to his life and death.

It's the Resurrection.

The claim that Jesus rose from the dead is absolutely ridiculous, viewed from the outside. That's where you get smug people calling him a Jewish Zombie. It's the tabloid lead story: "Man rises from the dead!"

But if there was ever an event that tethered the historical and the spiritual, it was the Resurrection.

The scholar Reza Aslan painted an interesting portrait of Jesus in his book, *Zealot: The Life and Times of Jesus of Nazareth*. He peels away the layers of religious caulk spackled upon Jesus. Aslan sees him essentially as a charismatic rebel against Rome who was brave enough to give up his life in a failed non-violent rebellion against Caesar.

As the scholar goes about his critical work, he pauses at the Resurrection. It's the place where we all get snagged as we read the Gospels and use our brains.

He says that you can't write much about it objectively because it was a subjective event. The risen Jesus didn't appear initially to non-believers but to those who were his followers. Aslan says it would be easy to dismiss the Resurrection as wishful thinking from his starry-eyed and disappointed disciples.

What stops him from making that assessment is what he calls a "nagging fact." He says that the people who said they had seen the risen Jesus were executed, sometimes in a grisly fashion, for what they claimed to have witnessed. It wasn't like they were heretics, asked to recant a belief they had. Rather, for these early Christians it was a matter of them being asked to deny what their eyes had clearly seen. You can't deny the risen sun in the sky and you can't deny the risen Jesus standing before you.

You can live as largely as you want, as Jesus of Nazareth did. But if he rose from the dead, I want to be 100% sure of it, because I'm not going to risk my life for a lie.

His followers were sure. And Paul, who admitted he was pretty obnoxious in his younger years, was sure as well. Encountering Jesus (Acts 9) moved his life onto a different trajectory. It propelled him with the energy of a central conviction: "For to me, living is Christ and dying is gain" (Philippians 1:21).

For him, as for others, the witness of the Resurrection cast aside any doubts about Jesus. He states this honestly.

> If Christ has not been raised, your faith is futile and you are still in your sins. Then those also who have died in Christ have perished. If for this life only we have hoped in Christ, we are of

all people most to be pitied. But in fact, Christ has been raised from the dead, the first fruits of those who have died.

(1 Corinthians 15:17-20)

Steve Jobs, the founder of Apple, had a unique effect on people. He seemed to embody an alternate reality, with visions of strange looking personal computers and of little rectangular devices containing incredible power. Additionally, you could use them to talk to people while they're displayed in pixel-brilliant color. Jobs wanted to make a dent in the universe and he presented a vision that made people think it was possible. People got caught up in the dream he projected.

At the baseline, Jesus had that same effect (and he was much nicer to be around). Only with him, there was the claim that such transcendence happened not only when you were around him pre-cross but also post-cross.

Such a claim confronts sense and sensibility.

Maybe that's the point.

The Resurrection means acknowledging there's a mysterious, unpredictable side to Jesus that you can't eliminate. Followers of his died before they would reduce him to being just a master teacher, a moral example or a good guy.

The Gospel writers are silent about the "how" of the Resurrection, which is what we 1's and 0's people would like. They eerily say that he sometimes appeared in a materializing/vanishing sort of way (Luke 24:31; John 20:19, 26), while at other times he enjoyed a breakfast of fish (John 21:9-10).

The "why" of the Resurrection is much clearer. If he is somehow alive, what are you going to do about it?

For me, I believe the Resurrection because it began my journey as a Christian and continues to play out in the storyline of my life.

I was fascinated by Jesus in adolescence. It led to what I felt was a personal encounter with him.

I've had experiences since that have made me stop and ponder things that seemed extraordinary, unexplainable by reason. That supports the out-of-the-ordinary encounter that started my spiritual journey. My background makes me link the transcendent to God, not just to an experience I simply can't explain at the moment.

I've lived in a community of faith where people share similar stories, both about experiencing Christ's presence and having transcendent moments outside of rationality.

I've explored his teachings and struggled with them. As I've tried to put them into practice, I've been amazed at how my connectedness to others and to the world deepens.

The above subjective life-narrative grounds me, fulfilling my need for security and identity.

Yet it comes with an uncomfortable tension between reason and mystery. You can obviously look at my personal story and blow holes in it rationally. At the end of the day (or my life, whichever comes first), there's that honest, rational nakedness that admits that all of the above could be a delusion.

This internal nudity constrains unwarranted arrogance. It keeps me questioning as honestly as I can, trying not to fall into the trap of confirmation bias, of seeing only what I want to see.

Yet, to deny the mysterious side of life that I've perceived and processed is to be equally dishonest. My testimony, being $1/7,000,000,000^{th}$ of the world's population, is that there is a texture to living that's much more than the rational alone, and it's linked to a personal God whom I experience through Jesus.

Maybe it comes down to a rational openness. I'd like to understand the reason behind things. I want and need to ask "Why?" But is it intellectually dishonest, or intellectually honest, to sometimes ask, "Why not?" That might open possibilities to see a more complete picture than what our limited rationalist perspective gives.

Perhaps my faith narrative related above connects with your story in some fashion. Perhaps it doesn't. Regardless, how we approach the irrational claim that Jesus transcends death reflects how we approach life in its totality.

Transcendent moments that confront us naturally point to the mysterious. The Resurrection is the capstone transcendent possibility, shaking our security in ourselves and our worldview.

It is, in the final reflection, like a teeter-totter. The mysterious is on one end and the rational on the other. The fulcrum is honesty and humility. To be fully human we should be in rhythmic motion between the two ends. If we stay grounded only on one side, we're going to be out of balance and won't have much fun.

This constant movement helps us see how a faith that feels right and makes sense could appear. It's one that doesn't diminish the tension between rationality and spirituality.

Also, such a faith might not be what you think it is.

Re-Constructing

"I have faith; help my lack of faith!"

--Mark 9:24

Chapter Eleven—*Faith Isn't What You Think It Is*

If you grew up in church, you were probably taught some of the historic creeds, such as the Apostles' or Nicene. These are statements that outline what the Christian faith is all about. If, without mental reservation or purpose of evasion, you can say you believe all those things, then you're in. You're part of the Christian fold.

This must be a huge turn-off to people inquiring about a faith that makes sense and feels right. Right off the bat it presents Christianity as an intellectual exercise. Suspend disbelief so you can believe.

The classic response, of course, is that you must have some standards. You can't just believe anything and call yourself a Christian. If you can't say part of the creed, then skip over it for the time being. Work on your belief system until you can join those who can recite it without crossed fingers.

This is not real helpful to skeptics.

A better response is expanding what we mean by faith.

Maybe faith is simply having the courage to seek a more complete story than the limited one your inner author is writing for you. Maybe it's having the unpretentiousness to look for a broader set of answers to your questions.

This way faith isn't just doing mental gymnastics. Rather, it's putting yourself out there, trusting there may be an underlying symmetry to this world that will sustain you. Maybe such work will be rewarded with a yellowy-golden type of experience. Maybe you'll be able to name the Mystery, or at least see its shadow.

To venture out like this is to have the intellectual, emotional and experiential honesty to confront the mysterious side of life without arrogantly or frightfully slamming the door because of what you might find.

The patron saint of someone who lived with such honesty was Leonarda Da Vinci.

Biographer Walter Isaacson is the latest to chronicle this Renaissance man. In his exhaustive book, Isaacson notes the wide range of interests that went along with his considerable artistic talents. Da Vinci did in-depth studies in engineering, science, anatomy, botany, aviation and ornithology.

The author didn't start his research with Da Vinci's art, but rather with his notebooks. More precisely, with more than 7,200 pages of his "notes and scribbles."

What those pages reveal is DaVinci's insatiable curiosity along with a meticulous eye for detail. He didn't take things for granted, but kept pressing with, "Why?" He questioned everything from "Why is the sky blue?" to "What does a woodpecker's tongue look like?"

Isaacson cites two quotes that sum up the Italian's character. Art historian Kenneth Clark: DaVinci is "the most relentlessly curious man in history." And art critic Adam Gopnik: "Leonardo remains weird, matchlessly weird, and nothing to be done about it."

Anyone who's seeking answers to life's mysteries should be worthy of those descriptors. Relentlessly curious. Matchlessly weird.

The spiritual life must be fueled by pushing the envelope and not caring how you appear in the process.

Why do I say, do and think the things I say, do and think?

How can I be sure I'm living in a way that honors who I am and, perhaps, what I should be doing with my life? And, who am I and how do I know what I should be doing with my life, anyway?

What do atheists teach me?

What do Christians teach me?

What do people of other faiths teach me? Do I even know people of other faiths, to begin with?

What do people at a stage of life different from my own teach me?

What do people having lifestyles and values different from my own teach me? What is my basis for judging them? Why would I want to judge them anyway?

What courses should I take, books should I read, people should I talk to, in order to get some insights into the areas with which I'm struggling?

Why do people post and tweet what they do? What are they afraid of? What am I afraid of?

Why am I a liberal? Why am I a conservative? Why do I use such labels?

Asking such questions leads to more questions. Like an archeological dig, you keep sifting through layers until you find a foundation that feels right to you and makes sense. Maybe (from my perspective) it will link you to your Creator. Maybe it won't, but at least you will have gained a wider perspective than before you started, and who knows where that will lead?

One thing is certain, however. You will not start your spiritual journey, you will not start digging into the soil of life, without the essential qualities of honesty and humility. Delusion and arrogance prevent curiosity and weirdness.

Let's narrow this to Jesus.

Paul, in one of his writings, gave a practical exercise in making faith a verb. He said, "Adopt the attitude that was in Christ Jesus" (Philippians 2:5).

If you studied Jesus' teachings, noted how he related to people, saw the things he did, what do you think would be his attitude?

What would be his attitude about your attitudes? Values? Relationships?

What would be his attitude about the ethics of your company?

What would be his attitude about our current political climate?

You can keep going with the "what would be" game, but it's a good illustration of faith as a process of discovery.

Who knows where the game will take you? Perhaps you'd feel a nudge to make some changes. Play it long enough and maybe classic Christian words—forgiveness, mercy, confession, hope—might take on modern meaning. Maybe some beliefs start forming that you can affirm with integrity. If so, they will be tailored to you.

Regardless of whether or not this leads you to a spiritual affirmation, being curious in and of itself is a faith stance you're taking in today's climate. People tweet words followed by periods, not question marks. They boast their certainties, not their curiosities.

To ask honest, humble questions is a game-changer, regardless of whether you land inside or outside the religious fold.

Da Vinci embodied curiosity and weirdness, honesty and humility. He created art that still enriches the world.

For this genius, though, his pushing the envelope was a lifelong endeavor. His contributions to the world didn't come over night, but slowly emerged as life honored his curiosity by opening up before him.

This type of tireless persistence was also the genius of the early church.

In the first century you couldn't read a book, take a class and join your local congregation. Rather, once you became curious about this weird off-shoot of Judaism, you began a process that could or could not result in you becoming a Christian. Sometimes it took up to three years before you joined, if ever.

During that period of time you were a student. You pursued your curiosity, asking questions and struggling with the answers. You were slowly instructed in early Christian thought as it was being formed (which took a while as well).

You were also required to alter your lifestyle. Living in the ancient Roman culture, you had a lot to alter if you were to conform to the bedrock values rising from the Christian faith. Issues of sexuality, slavery, the status of women, classism, idolatry, money and materialism were on the forefront. Did the way you conduct yourself in all aspects of your life reflect your new-found Christian values?

Only after the elders found you worthy in both understanding and lifestyle were you admitted into the church. You could then attend the full worship service, engage in the sacraments and participate in all aspects of congregational life.

There was a practical motive behind this "patient ferment," as church historian Alan Kreider expressed it. It assured the band of Christians you weren't a spy. It wasn't exactly popular to be part of this sect. Becoming a member of "The Way," as the movement was called, could have serious negative consequences for you, not the least of which was torture and death. (*The Patient Ferment of the Early Church*)

But it seems like there was a spiritual motive as well. The spiritual life is not an impatient life. It takes time to grow your soul. Affirmations of faith aren't simply to be given verbal endorsement and then you move on to the potluck. Rather, the spiritual life is a Da Vinci type of inquiry-fueled process up until the moment of your death. The patience of the early faith community reflected that.

There's a famous definition of faith in the New Testament: "Faith is the reality of what we hope for, the proof of what we don't see" (Hebrews 11:1). You receive that assurance and conviction not by mental manipulations. For the Christian, you receive it by actively questioning and testing out your answers within a faith community.

That's why it's important to make sure that a church grows, and not stunts, someone's quest for authentic faith.

Chapter Twelve—*The Church Isn't What You Think It Is*

From the very beginning of its history, and in the centuries since, there have been conflicts in the Christian community.

There were problems with widows in the early church, who went from house to house spreading gossip. There were zealous people who said you had to believe a certain way or they labeled you a heretic and did bad things to you. There were power struggles as new people came in with new ideas and charter members took offense. There were denominational battles over things ranging from how you should understand communion and baptism to whether certain types of people should have equal rights in church.

Yet, as someone who's seen parish pro's and con's for a few decades, I can affirm without hesitation that one of the things this world has going for it is this institution.

The church has helped the United States adhere to some of the basic values upon which it was founded. When the nation strayed from them, the church became a major voice in the national conscience and such things as the civil rights movement were birthed.

The church has been on the forefront of helping those marginalized in society. This stems from its morality and ethics, the fruits of faith. Even though atheists may disagree with that faith, some resonate with many of the values churches espouse, as Hemant Mehta has noted.

Personally speaking, the greatest, kindest and most generous people I've ever known are found in the church. They are grace-filled, forgive pastoral mistakes (I know this first-hand) and reach out with love, prayers and casseroles whenever someone goes through a difficult time.

It's been a privilege to know such people and to serve churches that have such folks in them.

However, all that is secondary to the point of this book.

How can a church be an ally, and not an obstacle, in the quest for a faith that makes sense and feels right?

First, last and foremost, the church fosters authentic faith <u>by dialoguing with diverse voices</u>.

If honesty and humility result in anything concrete, it's people with varying opinions (about faith, politics, whatever) sitting down and learning from each other. That learning takes place in worship, small groups, service activities, interfaith gatherings…anywhere they can meet.

The early church grew when it invited all to the table and didn't assign preferred seating. Jesus made a point of inclusivity in his church (Luke 14:7-24). He also identified with those you wouldn't ordinarily find sitting in the pew on a weekend (Matthew 25:31-46). It was as if a variety of voices clarified Jesus' voice, a variety of attitudes clarified Jesus' attitude.

Humility and honesty push parishioners to dialogue, and the more diverse the voices, the better. What are their life experiences and their wisdom? Studying the Scriptures with them can unveil different facets of Biblical jewels. Stretching the meaning of over-used terms like grace, forgiveness, righteousness, obedience, faith can reveal new insights. That's what Jesus did in his teachings.

For a church to stifle diverse voices is to engage in collective original sin.

We are all flawed, from birth to death. Our default nature is to listen to our inner storyteller and believe that story uncritically. And, like a gaggle of geese, we most naturally huddle together with those who agree with the plot and characters in our subconscious tales.

Salvation may turn us around and reconcile us to God, but it doesn't snuff out this fatal failing. We must work on it all our lives. That's why we need each other, to keep us accountable to honesty and humility.

We are, indeed, better together. Splitting off to form a congregation where people think alike is not what Jesus had in mind.

A congregation can best promote diverse voices <u>by embracing grace and exorcising (not exercising) judgment</u>.

There's a popular Jesus meme on the internet where he's teaching on a hillside, with a child on his lap, surrounded by people intently listening to him.

"So here is what I want you to do. Love others just as I have loved you. Take care of them and don't judge them."

Someone responds, "But what if they're gay, or worship other gods, or don't worship at all?"

Jesus answers the question with a question.

"Did I stutter?"

He didn't, and he's clear.

There is a great deal of difference between welcoming and condoning. Because you welcome someone doesn't mean you personally condone their attitudes or lifestyle. How could you? We all have different narratives running in our heads. Indeed, it's because we have different narratives that we need one another, to make our stories broader and more interesting.

A congregation should welcome all who seek a connection with God, or however they may call what they're seeking. Jesus' attitude is inclusive; after all, God so loved the *world*.

Perhaps we mistake welcoming for condoning because the security-loving part of us sometimes conjures up fear. Fear of the other is really fear that our inner storyline might not be true. Such fright is the indicator that love needs to kick in, for that is what drives it out (1 John 4:18). Having truly open hearts, minds and doors, as the old mantra of the United Methodist Church once stated, is a good start.

This welcoming spirit happens when Christians unite <u>by being persistently inquisitive</u>.

I believe God's love, grace, wisdom, values, desires are so vast and incomprehensible that we need to be relentlessly curious. There's always something to be surprised by, something new to discover.

There is revealed truth in the Bible, in the historic creeds, in traditions and theologies from past centuries. Such truth guides, informs, challenges.

There is also new knowledge we've gained over the last 2,000 or so years. Has God been silent during that time?

God's revelation in the past is foundational. The subsequent knowledge we've gained since helps bring out that wisdom. It helps translate that wisdom in new ways and deepen our understanding of what Jesus' attitude for today could be.

However, we'll never learn anything new, and we will not hear God's fresh voice, if we think we know it already. Asking challenging questions, and challenging convenient answers, keep us open.

If God loves the world, God continues speaking in many ways. Honesty and humility give us ears to hear, and those should be eager ears.

Speaking of the past, it's time now for an intermission.
Before continuing with thoughts about what a faith community can do today, let's look at a couple of things it did as it was forming.

First, no sooner was the church born than it took an aggressive stand against bigotry.

Since Christianity began as a Jewish sect, a problem arose when non-Jews were attracted to the church and became believers. The underlying issue was the pride that some original Christians felt in their Jewish heritage, which resulted in them treating these non-Jewish Christians as second-class. To press the matter, the Jewish Christian leaders demanded that those Gentiles first become Jewish before being admitted into full inclusion. This meant they had to observe rituals and, for the men, be circumcised (obviously a deal breaker for some guys).

In a show of counter-cultural force, the church stood up to this thinly-veiled bigotry. Ex-Jewish fisherman turned disciple, Simon Peter, made a bold speech:

> I really am learning that God doesn't show partiality to one group of people over another. Rather, in every nation, whoever worships him and does what is right is acceptable to him. This is the message of peace he sent to the Israelites by proclaiming the good news through Jesus Christ: He is Lord of all!
> (Acts 10:34-36)

This didn't sit too well with some of the Hebrew Christians, even if it did come from the man Jesus blessed as having the faith upon which the church would be built. They pressed their case to the Christian Supreme Court in Jerusalem. After hearing both sides, Chief Justice James (Jesus' brother) announced his verdict. "Therefore, I conclude that we shouldn't create problems for Gentiles who turn to God" (Acts 15:19).

It's difficult to underestimate the miracle those words reflected. Jews gave up their centuries-old prejudice against Gentiles.

Second, the early church made a concerted effort to challenge its surroundings.

Roman culture had little regard for human rights. Magic and religion intermingled. Rome boasted a pantheon of gods, with idolatry and emperor worship ruling the day. Violence backed up such worship, and if you crossed the ruling power you were executed on the cross or sent to the Coliseum for entertainment. The scientific/empirical worldview was nonexistent; not only was the earth the center of the cosmos, but Rome was the center of the center.

The social order reflected Rome's moral bankruptcy. Unwanted babies were discarded in garbage landfills. Slavery was justified and cruel treatment of the slaves endorsed. Women were second class citizens at best, and property at worst. There was a huge gulf between rich and poor.

The church structured itself in direct opposition to this climate. It was like a dam that grew taller, wider and thicker against the current.

The communal gatherings of those early Christians were guided by a rule of strict equality. Paul wrote, "There is neither Jew nor Greek; there is neither slave nor free; nor is there male and female, for you are all one in Christ Jesus" (Galatians 3:28). He expected the churches he led to follow that rule. When they gathered, the rich sat beside the poor. The slaves next to the masters. Men next to women. Ex-Jews next to Gentiles.

What's more, they focused not just on showing compassion to each other but also to those outside their Christian tribe.

Outbreaks of disease were common in the cities. Sometimes they resulted in full-blown plagues. When that happened, the healthy citizens isolated themselves from the diseased. They might not have known about bacteria and viruses but they knew that if you hung around the dying too long, you could end up in the morgue as well.

But what did those crazy Christians do? Instead of running away from the sick, they ran towards them. They tended to those others had abandoned.

All of this caught the attention of the populace. There was something tremendously appealing about such an egalitarian community that wasn't afraid to show edgy compassion to those outside that community.

There's a direct correlation between this and the rate of growth of Christianity. The church saw its strongest advance in its first three centuries of existence. Some scholars have speculated that there may have been as many as 5-6 million Christians by the time the religion was made legal in the 300's.

It seemed that people were intrigued by a community where they could learn about an alternate reality. They weren't rushed and they weren't judged. They had the grace to alter their lifestyle accordingly. In the process, the man Jesus seemed to take on flesh and blood before their very eyes; that might be why communion meant so much to them. The things they heard about him, as outlandish as they seemed at the beginning, began to make sense. Their heart informed their mind.

And they became believers.

The preceding scenes reveal an institution born to be counter-cultural. It's in its DNA. Proclaim unconditional love and express it in justice/empowerment for all, and you have an institution that can't be comfortable in society. It doesn't matter whether that society is in the first or the twenty-first century.

What does this say about how a group of people can shape belief?

A church fosters faith <u>by merging spiritual and social issues</u>.

Understanding things like humility, compassion, sacrifice, forgiveness only in interpersonal terms deprives them of their full power. Translate them also in terms of standing up to an arrogant, vengeful, degrading world, and they flex their muscle.

The spiritual and the social are intertwined. You can't talk about a kingdom of God without talking about how the kingdom of the world is opposed to it. The early church lived in constant tension with the authorities, which was because of Jesus' message. The Caesar vs. Christ conflict was a zero-sum game.

The easy road for modern congregations, lest they be accused of meddling, is to proclaim a message that focuses on doing things that will make you happy now and get you into heaven later. Such a message abdicates to the powers of the world that killed Jesus.

Confront them or resign to the executioners.

The church fosters faith <u>by presenting an alternative vision</u>.

Even though confrontation with society produces conflict, the goal is a society where all, enemy and friend, can come together in peace. There will be no prisoners of war. The tools the Christian uses, as we'll see in a later chapter, ensure a different kind of victory.

Meanwhile, bumper-sticker mentality rages, fueled by social media. Hostile caricatures are painted of liberals, conservatives, immigrants, LGBTQ, elites, working class, Muslims, Jews, blacks, Latinos, Asians...fill in the blank. Heated stereotypes trigger tribal reactions. Our imagined, tweeted fears sometimes even compel us to mix faith with nationalism and politics.

It's easy to forget that in all of this, we're still those minuscule specks who really don't know what we're talking about. Such humility should shatter the imagined walls we build to make us feel secure.

A faith community should embody and promote a vision where we don't have anything to fear from each other. Indeed, it should be a community where we have everything to gain from each other.

When Dr. King dreamed of the children of former slaves and former slave owners sitting around the dinner table, he was painting but one scene of the timeless vision of the church. We just need to keep adding scenes for each generation.

We keep translating that vision <u>by living as if actions are truly louder than words</u>.

It wasn't so much the words that catalyzed the early church for growth as it was their actions. How striking to have seen Christians nursing plague victims at great risk to themselves. Those life-savers might have mightily disagreed with each other on their understanding of communion, but they agreed on what was essential: self-sacrificial love on behalf of another, even a pagan stranger.

Words, over-spoken or over-written, can facilitate argument and division. Acts of justice, mercy and compassion, both internal and external, go a long way in not only uniting but in educating. Concepts of God are sometimes best explained in actions, not sermons. Maybe the best theology comes from action then reflection. Jesus always backed up what he said by healing, feeding, consoling, confronting and forgiving.

Having painted the above portrait of the ideal faith community, it's obvious that it's just that. An ideal.

Like people, a congregation should embody honesty and humility. Each succeeds, and fails, in its own way. And like someone searching for meaning as best they can, each congregation should be cut some slack.

Sincere believer and sincere non-believer alike can profit from a faith community that tries to approximate the above ideals. It's the environment necessary to enrich your search. Giving a congregation a chance might open you to a transcendent moment that could help guide you on your own unique path. It might lead you to a semblance of faith that makes sense and feels right.

Or, it might lead you to affirm that you can't believe in a higher power right now. You walked through the church door, giving it your best shot, and found that it was best for you to walk right back out of it, not caring to return in the foreseeable future.

Since faith is a verb, you engaged in it. The very fact that your honesty and humility may have led you to seek a congregation of equally honest and humble people counts for something. You will have had experiences through following your curiosity that will stick with you. Who knows what will happen in the future? We do live in a world of mystery, right?

Your church journey comes with no authentic faith guarantee. Regardless, though, your journey will have taken you to a point where you might find an old book speaking in a new way.

Earlier I documented the fragmentation critics can point to regarding the Bible.

It's time now to run a defragging program.

Chapter Thirteen—*A Different Take on the Bible*

As I'm writing, there's a bit of angst in my denomination, the United Methodist Church. The issue is what our stance on LGBTQ should be. The church's traditional position has been exclusion: no same sex marriage and no ordination of self-avowed, practicing homosexuals. This point is being strongly challenged. A showdown is coming.

The resulting polarization is extremely painful. It's brought out the worst in some ways and validates objections outsiders have of the church.

There is, though, a tiny sliver of good that's emerging.

People are having to take a deeper look at the Bible.

How do you, should you, read it?

One staunch traditionalist, objecting to inclusion, counseled that in the midst of this turmoil we should remain "rooted and grounded" in God's Word.

I take that to mean that if something is prohibited in the Bible, as homosexual relations appear to be in some places, then we would be wise to obey. Otherwise, we will be swayed by human teaching instead of divine. To cave on this issue is to open the door to secular humanism, and then the Gospel is compromised all over the place.

But is that what the phrase "rooted and grounded" should mean? You honor God's Word by pointing to words on a page?

That seems pretty defensive.

As we've seen, we already override some things. Rationality combined with sensitivity softens literalism, for most. How do you determine when to enforce one prohibition (homosexuality) and relent on others (don't eat pork, don't divorce)? How do you choose which laws to accept? Which do you ignore because they're outdated or hurtful?

Additionally, playing the "it's in the Bible" game ignites more arguments than it settles.

One of the larger controversies our nation faced in the spring of 2018 was the zero-tolerance enforcement of the immigration policy. This resulted in the forced separation of children from their illegal-immigrant parents.

The outcry against this atrocity came swiftly. It even united some Republicans and Democrats, which is a small miracle in itself.

During the fallout, the Attorney General at that time, Jeff Sessions, employed an interesting defense strategy. He quoted the Bible, citing Paul's words in Romans 13.

It was a religious landmine that blew up in his face.

It is very easy to use the Bible to justify something. When you want to defend a position that's important to you, the Bible is a handy source. There are over 31,000 verses in the Old and New Testaments. You are certain to find a few that will say what you want them to say. As noted earlier, people once used portions of the Bible to justify slavery and misogyny. Sanctioning actions and attitudes through cut-and-paste verses gives an appearance of divine approval.

The tricky thing about this is that opponents can cite counter passages. For every Romans 13:1a ("Every person should place themselves under the authority of the government") there's an Exodus 22:21a ("Don't mistreat or oppress an immigrant").

There must be a better way to approach Scripture.

For me, being rooted and grounded in God's Word means four interrelated things.

The first is <u>hearing the witness of the Biblical writers as they express themselves within their own times and settings</u>.

As we've already seen, the Bible is a collection of works written over the course of 1,000 years. Getting to know the authors, their culture and their time period helps you see things through their eyes. You gain an understanding of what is essential and true from their perspective. Some things will definitely rise to the surface as speaking to their setting, not ours (see: Leviticus). But many other things will shine light on the issues pressing us today.

The Rev. Adam Hamilton, in his book *Making Sense of the Bible*, has done an excellent job in detailing three types of Biblical passages. The majority reflect the "timeless will of God" for us. A second grouping reflects God's will for a specific period of time. A final bucket of passages doesn't reflect God's will but rather historical/cultural ideas.

It takes work and study to do what Hamilton advocates. It means getting acquainted with the people and the cultures behind book, chapter and verse.

The payoff is worth it.

When you allow the Bible to breathe by not thinking that every verse is equal to every other verse, carrying identical importance and relevance for today, you begin to see things differently. You notice remarkably consistent themes. Compassion. Sin and forgiveness. Faith and trust. Grace. Righteousness. Justice. Obedience. Sacrifice. Humility. Freedom. Reverence. They are all there, hung like laundry blowing in the wind between the poles of the Ten Commandments and the Sermon on the Mount.

What's more, there's an amazing consistency in the major narrative of the Bible. In the midst of many minor and conflicting tales, there's a united one. God made a good earth. God is pro-people. People are anti-God. God doesn't give up trying to turn that "anti" into "pro." God reveals the divine heart in Jesus, once and for all. When we seek God with a curiosity rising from honesty and humility, our lives will be transformed. We'll follow God's lead instead of our own, and work for God's big kingdom instead of our own little one.

This is how I understand the Bible to be inspired. Only God's working behind the scenes could produce such unswerving motifs and storyline. Given the chaos of the millennium in which it was written, this is a wonder.

Celebrating this uniformity is affirming the inspiration of Scripture. It's the fruit of seriously studying the Bible without minds and hearts already made up. We're working the Word to hear the Spirit.

Being rooted and grounded in God's Word also means <u>approaching Scripture with intense curiosity and openness</u>. You should let your inner Da Vinci out to play and let the playground be spacious.

The preceding chapter gave practical tips for seeking out a congregation that will help birth and nurture a faith instead of still-birthing it. Maybe it would be helpful here to add some practical questions if you decide to do a little Bible study. When you're pondering a passage, be curious. Ask yourself:

Would Jesus agree with this writer?

Does the writer have a bias contrary to what Jesus would say?

Does the passage make sense?

Does it agree with my experiences or run counter to them?

Is this one of the major themes in the Bible? What are those themes?

If the passage says something is a sin, why is it a sin? What's my understanding of sin, and why?

Does the passage have a parallel somewhere else in the Bible? If so, is there a difference?

Am I getting uneasy by what I'm reading? Why?

Am I feeling affirmed by what I'm reading? Why?

What do other people, dead or alive, think about this passage?

It's mystical to me how life deepens when you approach this ancient book with such reverence. In religious terms, you're opening the door for the Spirit to pass through.

The honest questions you ask may result in responses of grace, comfort and direction, perhaps when you are at your most vulnerable. For example, discovering God speaking to you the words once spoken to Israel can be transformational.

> I know the plans I have in mind for you, declares the LORD; they are plans for peace, not disaster, to give you a future filled with hope (Jeremiah 29:11).

> Don't fear, for I have redeemed you; I have called you by name; you are mine. When you pass through the waters, I will be with you; when through the rivers, they won't sweep over you. When you walk through the fire, you won't be scorched and flame won't burn you (Isaiah 43:1b-2).

On the other hand, your openness to Scripture could result in making you nervous. The Bible has the knack of critiquing more of our actions than condoning them.

When we ask questions of the Biblical witnesses, they can ask questions in return. How well do our words and actions unify, instead of divide? How well do we seek to understand before posting or tweeting? How well do we stand in solidarity with victims of discrimination, fear and violence? How well do we advocate for access to better schools and healthcare?

This grilling can upset the status quo and undermine political agendas. Again, the Scriptures know no separation between spiritual and social issues. You cannot read the Bible with integrity and not expect to be confronted as well as comforted.

For atheist or believer, bringing such curiosity to what you're reading is important common ground. I personally believe that the Spirit will find a home in all who approach the Bible with honesty, humility and openness. Whether or not you can name that Spirit at this point in your journey may really be beside the point. If God does exist, God will understand a person's limitation in knowing and naming the deity. God will honor the attempt of the person to seek a deeper side of life, one that helps others and makes this world a more beautiful place.

Third, being rooted and grounded in God's Word means <u>interpreting Scripture through the eyes of Jesus.</u>

Marcus Borg, of yellowy-golden transcendent experiences fame, said that Jesus should be the standard by which to understand the rest of the Bible. His mission and message form the Rosetta Stone, the translating tool, of the texts. Jesus opens up the insights hiding just under the written words. (*Convictions*)

From this perspective, we don't get hung up so much on "Did this happen or did someone just have a really vivid imagination?" The truth lies in the overall story itself and the validation of that truth lies in contemporary living. God intervened in human history. Jesus is the ultimate intervention. From that event, backward and forward, Scripture speaks with a Jesus accent for the Christian.

Accordingly, of all the Bible study questions we can ask, the first two listed earlier are foundational. Would Jesus agree with this writer? Does the writer have a bias contrary to what Jesus would say?

For the atheist, though, interpreting the Scriptures through the Jesus lens probably doesn't make a whole lot of sense. If you're not starting from such a vantage point, the Scriptures may still appear archaic and contradictory.

However, this way of reading the Bible does address a complaint that non-believers have.

Remember the 613 laws of the Pharisees? Conventional wisdom says that the Bible is a rule book. It's easy to focus on the negative ones. It's easiest of all to fall into the self-righteous trap of separating saint from sinner based on the particular laws that suit the interpreter's outlook.

This is a tremendous turn-off for non-believers. It also gives angry televangelists good fodder for finger pointing.

Filtering Scripture through Jesus' message eliminates this. From this perspective, the Bible isn't a book on law but a book about love, specifically how to express Jesus' love in the current context of the reader.

Some will raise the point that once you start questioning what's in some Biblical sections, using "love your neighbor as yourself" type criteria, then you've lost objective standards. Where will it end?

Why not see?

Wouldn't it be lovely to see us overdo the loving-as-Jesus-loved-without-stuttering thing, for a change?

Finally, being rooted and grounded in God's Word means studying it with people who see things differently.

If the church fosters faith by dialoguing with different voices, as we've seen, then that can be expressed in the nitty gritty of studying the Bible in such a way that those voices can be heard.

It's been my experience that when churches form Bible study groups, they often tag them according to type. There's a conservative group, a liberal group, a social issues group, a young adults group, a parenting group...the smorgasbord can be quite bountiful. They all approach Scripture from different perspectives.

Such clusters are needed. They're good connecting points for people. "Like attracts like" is not a bad rule for the beginning of a person's journey in a faith community.

That journey truly deepens, though, when you introduce some diversity.

It would be very refreshing to use some hot-button topics to foster true dialogue instead of divisive argument.

What does the Bible say about homosexuality? Why not have a special study that contains members from the LGBTQ community?

What about racism? Why not have a special study that is multi-racial?

What about ageism? Why not have a special study that is multi-generational?

As long as we bring the right attitude to the table, we can and should welcome a variety of voices around that table. One of the fruits of discussing with diverse voices is that there's room for disagreement. As long as honesty and humility characterize our discussions, we can stay together and be better for it. We can each believe what we believe because we remember that we're still those microscopic specks clinging to a grain of sand planet spinning in an infinite cosmos. Our positions on any issue will always be relative and subjective. We need each other to help us see the larger view.

For example, the United Methodist church, in the way it handles the issue of human sexuality, has a golden opportunity to reflect this inclusive attitude.

From my study, prayer and reflection, I believe that the Biblical places where homosexuality is prohibited belong in Hamilton's second bucket. They were meant for a different time period, within a different cultural context, and not today.

There are also people who hold the opposite view. They have taken the Bible equally seriously, they've studied and reflected, and have come to believe those passages belong in the first bucket.

Why should we be surprised at such disagreement? We all come from different perspectives. Such divergences are opportunities for us to continue dialoguing with each other, trusting that God is working in the background. They are also opportunities for us to show mutual respect, acknowledging we're all in this together as fellow flawed seekers.

Walking away from the table because you disagree, as advocated by my traditionalist colleague noted at the beginning of this chapter, is a reaction of fear. Remember: you don't diddle with someone's security, you don't suggest an alternative story line, without there being drastic reactions.

On the other hand, staying at the table with one another while you disagree is a sign of spiritual security. Honesty and humility allow the table of fellowship to keep adding new sections and chairs.

This will happen if we truly stay rooted and grounded in God's Word.

The Christian scriptures conclude with the Book of Revelation, a writing that is baffling to modern culture (and me). There is a lot of discussion on what various parts of it mean. The one thing that most people agree with is that the theme is "Jesus wins in the end." It's the vision that after the final struggle between good and evil, the reign of God will triumph and there will be a life where all those words in the Bible (compassion, justice, love, etc.) become realities with no qualifiers or disclaimers.

If we were to translate such a final vision into specific terms today, what would it look like?

It would be one where honesty and humility produce a harvest. In that vision, anyone who shares those qualities, regardless of whether or not they claim/name God, will be at home.

Chapter Fourteen—*A Different Vision*

Here's an interesting take on a famous New Testament story.

There's an incident where Jesus asks his disciples who they think he is. After some politically correct answers, Simon blurts out, "You are the Messiah, the Son of the living God" (Matthew 16:13-20). Jesus blesses him, renames him "The Rock" (where we get the name Peter), and says that he'll build his church on that rock. Hence, Peter is the first pope, and the papal succession train chugs out of the station.

There are, though, some unanswered questions regarding this.

For one, Jesus makes a point of going to a place called Caesarea Philippi for this dramatic encounter. That was a 32-mile round trip out of his way, just so this one thing could happen. Wouldn't it have been possible for him to ask his question and let the disciples respond without having to go on such an extended hike?

And second, what really does Jesus mean by renaming his disciple then saying that he's going to build a church on that rock? Mark's account of the story (8:27-30) doesn't mention this; the writer simply goes straight to the ending where Jesus orders the disciples not to tell anyone about his identity.

Digging into the historical context of the passage opens up things.

Caesarea Philippi was a Gentile area that had a strong Roman influence. There was a cave where it was believed that Pan, the god of the forests, lived. Inside the cave was a large sinkhole filled with water; some thought this was the entrance to Hades, the mythological underworld.

In front of such a sacred cave, then, it was only right that a temple should be built that honored Pan, along with other pagan deities. Google "temple of Pan," click images, and you'll see the remnants of the temple along with renderings of how it appeared. Quite impressive, but not surprising since the puppet king Philip enhanced it as a tribute to Caesar.

Jesus leads his disciples into this little taste of Roman culture in northern Palestine. There's a bustle of activity with people milling around, singing, dancing, worshipping.

Against such a backdrop, there's not a lot of added work needed for theatrical effect. You can envision Jesus stopping in front of the temple to the pagan god, chatting with his students, then delivering the punch line: "And I tell you, you are Peter, and on this rock, I will build my church, and the gates of Hades will not prevail against it" (Matthew 16:18).

Cue the drama. Jesus blesses Simon's declaration; it's that type of faith that anchors the church. And where will that church be built? "On this rock," and you can imagine Jesus pointing down to the ground, right in front of Pan's temple, which is the gateway to the underworld.

Jesus throws down the gauntlet. His church confronts Caesar's church. His kingdom goes toe to toe with the Roman king's. Which will prevail?

There is just no getting around that imagery of the church being the confronter of culture.

The challenge to anyone who is curious about Jesus might hear these questions from him: "Are you willing to risk your comfort for the sake of a greater cause? Are you willing to help me stare down the powers that break people and tried to break me?"

A good follow-up passage to the Caesarea Philippi one is Jesus' farewell conversation in John 13-17. He's giving his last lecture to his disciples. There's a tinge of sadness in his words because, well, it *is* farewell. Tomorrow he's going to be crucified. He'll never walk with them again in Palestine like he used to.

But it's more than a sermon. It's a motivational speech similar to a general giving a pep talk to the troops before battle. He says he chose each of them personally for this engagement. He tells them they're going to be in for a rough time because they've aligned themselves with him. The "ruler of this world" (the forces of evil, such as Rome) will be after them. They're not to lose heart, though. Unlike a general who stays well behind the front lines during battle, Jesus will be with them, side by side. He then clinches the speech, before a closing prayer, with this:

> I've said these things to you so that you will have peace in me. In the world you have distress. But be encouraged! I have conquered the world. (John 16:33)

It's right there. "In the world you have distress." Not prosperity. Not political power. Not assurance that everything will be OK.

In the midst of his speech, he also arms them for the fight. There will be one tool:

This is my commandment: love each other just as I have loved you. No one has greater love than to give up one's life for one's friends. You are my friends if you do what I command you.
(John 14:12-14)

Jesus is addressing his disciples when he's talking about friends. I wonder, though. Would it be a stretch to imagine that Jesus could also be referring to the ones who will be putting him and his disciples to death?

For Jesus, friends include enemies. Remember his other big teachings? Pray for enemies. Love, care and sacrifice for them. Forgive them. All those are the things we do for friends. And the ones confronting us are to be treated as friends in disguise.

Leave it to Jesus to tear down the basic human defense mechanism of labeling, dividing, stereotyping. There will be no more us and them, friend and enemy. There will only be friend.

This was a game changer in the building of Jesus' church on the rock opposite Pan's. Rome was all about dividing. Jesus is all about uniting, "that we may be one." Rome was about conquering through force. Jesus is about conquering through crazy love.

The "Christian soldier" is one who looks for people to call friend. The Christian starts on the fringe. Who is hurting? The immigrant? The gay couple? The elderly? The transgender? The Muslim or Jew? The inner city black or Latino? The Medicaid person? The developmentally challenged? The …?

What are they feeling? What do they need? What can you do?

The Christian moves on to the main stream. Who is deceived by the powers of this world? The racist? The homophobe? The materialist? The ageist? The redneck? The white collar? The …?

What are they feeling? What do they need? What can you do?

The way we build Jesus' church is to feel what others are feeling and connect with them as Jesus would. Guts in standing up for the one society condemns, like Jesus did for the woman caught in adultery. Guts in calling out hypocrisy and hate, like Jesus did in confronting the Pharisees. Guts in forgiving the ones who want to kill you, like Jesus did in absolving the soldiers nailing him to the cross.

When you eliminate enemy from your vocabulary and only see a friend, you've not just won a battle, but you've won the war. In one sense the conflict is over already. That's why the Book of Revelation might be redundant.

Of course this overlooks the bigger battle for the Christian soldier. The tougher contest is the internal one we must fight in order to reach the point of treating a former enemy as a present friend.

You can truly empathize with someone only after you swallow a large dose of humility.

Our need for security erects and thickens the wall between us and them. As long as such arrogance lives and breeds in our hearts, then anyone who calls themselves a believer in a just and loving God is a hypocrite.

Therefore, we are all hypocrites. I will admit it, front and center.

I confess that there's the knee-jerk instinct in me to confront someone who's being tacky with an, "Oh yeah?" I most naturally don't want to understand the person. I want to make sure that person understands how tacky they are being.

I need to work on that.

Like I need to dig deeper and confess that I can say we need to love the oppressor as well as the oppressed but, honestly, I really don't know what it's like to be oppressed. I'm a white male who's never had to fear discrimination in getting either the education or the job I want. Moreover, I've probably contributed unknowingly to oppression in thoughtless words or actions.

Again, I need to work on that.

Establishing the vision of Jesus' church isn't just an outward battle but, at the same time, an inner one. Humility indeed is a slippery virtue, mostly because our inner storyteller wants to write it out of our narrative.

We can only empathize with persons when we truly connect with them on an even playing field. Forging a humble heart levels that terrain.

When former enemies become friends, it's the most beautiful scene in the world, a little glimpse of what Jesus said was possible.

While writing this chapter, I saw a dramatic encounter between a former Neo-Nazi and a Jewish congregation. As of this writing, you can find it on YouTube under "Life After Hate: Tshuvah of a White Supremacist." St. Louis Post-Dispatch columnist Aisha Sultan gave a synopsis of it in her stltoday.com article on July 6, 2018.

Tony McAleer, 50, tells of how he'd been a skinhead since he was 15, when he encountered a group of young people brandishing swastikas. He bonded with them, not so much because of the hate rhetoric but because of the sense of purpose and support he felt. He said, "I had so much invested in this identity. It wasn't about whether I was correct."

At the same age I found Jesus, he found a group of Neo-Nazis. The adolescent need for security was met in both of us.

He became a zealous advocate of the hate philosophy. He was a face for them, even giving an occasional TV interview.

As he matured and gained life experiences, he saw the skinhead movement for what it was. It wasn't a matter of simply leaving it. It was dealing with the scars that the philosophy of hate had left, both in his soul and on the ones he'd hurt.

He sought out a therapist who, ironically, was Jewish. The counselor helped Tony unpack his considerable emotional baggage. Part of the healing process was to make amends with the groups he'd damaged.

That's why he returned to the Jewish congregation in his hometown of Vancouver, British Columbia. He had vandalized their synagogue decades before. He now had returned to face the consequences of his past. He wanted to express his anguish over what he had done. He explained to them that "there's no academic way of making someone compassionate. It happens through experience."

He made a point that he wasn't asking forgiveness. "I don't know if I had the right to ask for forgiveness."

At the conclusion of his remarks, though, it was obvious that he'd received that grace anyway. The handshakes and hugs proved it.

Note that the name Jesus and the label Christian weren't used in that story.

But was Jesus there in that synagogue? Was Jesus rejoicing? Was Jesus saying, "Take THAT, Rome!"?

In the end, we may not agree on terminology. "God" or "Nothing"? "Jesus as Savior" or "Jesus as Good Guy?" But when we join as one in honesty, humility and empathy, transcendent moments will happen that make life more beautiful than we imagine. As Tony said, we do gain compassion through experience.

Whether we name him or not in our human limitations, I believe such moments connect us to the Christ who is beyond our comprehension and manipulation. That is my belief, and it's the highest praise I could give him.

Faith in God, or lack thereof, may be an intensely personal and individualistic thing. What's not individualistic is the call to a higher cause that heals and not hurts, that empowers and not oppresses.

In that, we must all be one. And, in that larger sense, we all have the capability to claim the spirit behind the name Christian.

Albert Schweitzer expressed this best as he closed his work detailing his search for faith:

> He comes to us as One unknown, without a name, as of old, by the lake-side, He came to those men who knew Him not. He speaks to us the same word: "Follow thou me!" and sets us to the tasks which He has to fulfil for our time. He commands. And to those who obey Him, whether they be wise or simple, He will reveal Himself in the toils, the conflicts, the sufferings which they shall pass through in His fellowship, and, as an ineffable mystery, they shall learn in their own experience Who He is.
>
> *--Quest for the Historical Jesus*

Chapter Fifteen—*A Brief Conclusion*

It does indeed feel like yesterday when I left the ICU following Bobby's death and journeyed into that dark Atlanta morning.

I sometimes wonder why I didn't just check out from the God thing, given that horrific experience. Forget the third year of seminary. Join the management training program at Sears, which was a thing back then.

While I was in the process of slamming that door on God, though, I caught it just before it latched. It just didn't feel right to shut and bolt it. Was it fear? Security?

Maybe, in retrospect, it was discovering what a real relationship was supposed to be.

When we love someone, we also love how that person makes us feel. They fulfill needs we have. We want to protect that relationship. Consequently, we may inadvertently say or do things in order to exert some control over the beloved. Seminary professor Kate Bowler succinctly described the need for control as a drug to which we're all addicted. (*Everything Happens for a Reason*)

Breakthrough points in a relationship are when you refuse that narcotic. You dare let the other person be the other person, even though that may rattle your security cage.

Retrospectively, my shaking a fist at God was a good thing. It cleared the way for a more open relationship, not one where I tried to influence things by being pious and expecting warm feelings in return. If I was fully human with God, anger and all, God could be fully God with me.

We all have such pivotal events that stop us, shake us, and push us to ponder what just happened. Those events can be celebratory or, like Bobby's, filled with anguish.

The one thing they have in common, though, is that each is a chapter in the book you're continuing to write. To think your book only has one theme is like writing one long chapter. Such work is confusing to you and a bit boring to the reader.

The little storyteller in your head should consider all the events in your unique life, all the chapters, before saying, "This is who I am and what I believe." If your internal storyteller feeds you that line, talk back to it with, "This is who I am and what I believe, *at this point in my life.*"

Bobby's death chapter in my book was preceded by many other episodes. Some of them include Mother's dying when I was 4. Being raised in rural Missouri and appreciating the astounding beauty of nature. Encountering Jesus. Loving science because of a wonderful high school chemistry/physics teacher who happened to be an atheist. Being taught all things religious in college and seminary while meeting people from different backgrounds with different views.

After Bobby's death chapter, 40 plus years added many more. Encountering diverse people and experiences in church and out. Saying goodbye to Dad and other loved ones. Falling in love and transitioning from single to married status. Having kids. Going places. Discovering your body doesn't last forever.

When I read all those chapters, I'm not quite as disturbed by deep, unanswerable questions. Perhaps that's because so many things have happened that are beyond my comprehension that it's taught me my place in the universe. Very small. Very insignificant. Very grateful. Very transient.

Perhaps anyone who stops and creates chapter headings for their life's book might feel the same way.

In the end, we're all very flawed yet incredibly graced people. The line between sincere atheist and sincere believer can certainly be very thin. We're each writing our own small tome to add to the library of all those people who have written, and are writing, theirs.

We shouldn't diminish our work by including lots of labels in the chapters, either describing ourselves or others.

Honesty and humility should always safeguard us from this, since they remind us of who we really are.

They should also set our vision.

Several years ago I took my daughter to my hometown of Poplar Bluff, to visit the places she'd heard me talk about so often. Our first stop was the farm where I'd spent my teen years.

Getting out of the car, I was stunned. Nothing, *nothing*, appeared as I had remembered. The house was in disrepair. Trees had been so thinned out that you could see the next property. The lake had been reduced to just a large watering hole, and its shoreline was overgrown.

"Was this where all the stuff you talked about happened, Daddy?" Emma asked.

"Yes," I replied, "and no."

It became apparent that all the stories from the past, all the chapters I've written, exist exclusively in memory. They're phantoms I glimpse only through my mind's eye.

But looking down at Emma and holding her hand, I realized that, special as memories are, they are no substitute for the joys and challenges of the present, along with the hope for an unseen future.

There are always new chapters for each of us to write. How we live today will shape the content.

Without honesty and humility, our chapters will continue being written out of fear and characterized by delusion.

With honesty and humility, we will open ourselves to new possibilities, with new characters and subplots

That will make for a much more interesting read.

In the process, we might finally come to be at peace with the mystery we call life.

Epilogue—*In The Shadow of Mountains*

Reno, Nevada, is near some astoundingly beautiful scenery.

Within a short drive you can glide on mountains that take your breath away. The ski runs at the resorts give you unforgettable panoramas, especially those that curve around Lake Tahoe.

Some who fly into Reno, though, never make it to the mountains. Their destination is the casinos.

The gambling resorts offer different scenery. Glitz. Flashing lights. Blaring music. Garishly lit signs promising fantastic payouts. Surly looking women guarding their slots. Deadly-serious looking men seated around Texas Hold'em tables. Blackjack dealers with bored, glazed stares. Cocktail waitresses shilling drinks to keep the craps patrons happy and limber.

What a contrast.

The mountains envelop you in transcendent splendor. According to your perspective on things, some call the mountains the place where Creator and created meet.

The casinos are fashioned as a world unto themselves, fenced in by human passions and greed. We can seemingly be happy living in the highs and lows they artificially create. A manic-depressive sort of happiness.

We live our everyday lives in a casino-like world of our own creation. We pay the price as our emotional, physical, spiritual and national health lurches from crisis to crisis.

All the while, we live in the shadow of mountains that we don't often notice.

If the sea calls us to remember our past, then the mountains call us to envision our future. Maybe we are meant to partner with the Creator of this one-of-a-kind-in-the-universe ball of life. Maybe we're meant to make our planet even more unique by helping make it more beautiful. Maybe we are each created to pursue higher callings rather than lower desires.

The trick is not to get caught up in the flatlands between sea and mountain.

See you on the slopes.

Bibliography

Aslan, Reza. *Zealot: The Life and Times of Jesus of Nazareth*. Random House.

Barna, George. *Churchless: Understanding Today's Unchurched and How to Connect with Them*. Tyndale.

Bowler, Kate. *Everything Happens for a Reason, And Other Lies I've Loved*. Random House.

Brotherton, Rob. *Suspicious Minds: Why We Believe Conspiracy Theories*. Bloomsbury Sigma.

Collins, Frances. *The Language of God*. Free Press.

Eagleman, David M. *Incognito: The Secret Lives of the Brain*. Pantheon Books.

Freud, Sigmund. *Future of an Illusion*. W. W. Norton and Company.

Gushee, David P. *Still Christian: Following Jesus Out of American Evangelicalism*. Westminster John Knox Press.

Haidt, Jonathan. *The Happiness Hypothesis: Finding Modern Truth in Ancient Wisdom*. Basic Books.

Haidt, Jonathan. *The Righteous Mind: Why Good People Are Divided by Politics and Religion*. Pantheon Books.

Hamilton, Adam. *Making Sense of the Bible: Rediscovering the Power of Scripture Today*. HarperOne.

Harari, Yuval Noah. *Sapiens: A Brief History of Humankind*. Harper Collins.

Hitchens, Christopher. *God Is Not Great: How Religion Poisons Everything*. Grand Central Publishing.

Isaacson, Walter. *Da Vinci*. Simon and Schuster.

James, William. *The Varieties of Religious Experience*. Simon and Schuster.

Junger, Sebastian. *Tribe: On Homecoming and Belonging*. Twelve.

Korngold, Rabbi Jamie S. *The God Upgrade: Finding Your 21st-Century Spirituality in Judaism's 5,000-Year-Old Tradition*. Jewish Lights Publishing.

Kreider, Alan. *The Patient Ferment of the Early Church*. Baker Academic.

Mehta, Hemant. *I Sold My Soul on Ebay: Viewing Faith Through an Atheist's Eyes*. Waterbrook Press eBooks.

Nye, Bill. *Undeniable: Evolution and the Science of Creation*. St. Martin's Press.

Pollan, Michael. *How to Change Your Mind: What the New Science of Psychedelics Teaches Us About Consciousness, Dying, Addiction, Depression, and Transcendence*. Penguin Press.

Rohr, Richard. *The Naked Now*. Crossroad Publishing.

Russell, Bertrand. *Why I Am Not a Christian*. Touchstone.

Schweitzer, Albert. *Quest for the Historical Jesus*. The Project Gutenberg E-Book.

Singer, Michael. *The Untethered Soul: The Journey Beyond Yourself*. New Harbinger Publications, Inc.

Taylor, Jill Bolte. *My Stroke of Insight: A Brain Scientist's Personal Journey*. Viking Adult.

Wallace, Paul. *Stars Beneath Us*. Fortress Press.

Williams, Matt. "New model predicts that we're probably the only advanced civilization in the observable universe." www.phys.org, 6/22/18.

__Appendix A__

In Chapter Nine I told stories ranging from crosses in fields to mysterious black labs. According to your perspective, these were coincidences of things that just happen or they are calling cards from a deeper side of life. From the story-telling part of my brain, I believe the latter.

I asked folks in my congregation what tales they might tell of incidents in their lives that made them pause.

Here are some interesting ones.

From a Grateful Wife of a Police Officer

Last winter when the weather was really bad (icy conditions), he was driving to work. The only drivers on the road were police officers and salt trucks. He was at the stoplight when he realized that he hadn't put on his wedding ring from working out. (He never takes off his ring, but this particular time he did.)

He reached in the back to get his bag. He noticed the stoplight turn green. Because no one was behind him, he paused to grab the ring and put it on. Then, as he lifted his head to go, TWO huge trucks went sliding (could NOT stop) through the stoplight. If he would have gone at the moment the light turned green, he would have been hit.

From an Amazed Traveler

A few years ago, my sister and I were taking our yearly vacation together, and we were driving [from St. Louis] to the Destin area of Florida. On the second day of the drive, we pulled into a small Alabama town on a county road to go to McDonalds. We were only there to make a rest stop. We were walking towards the entrance and just going into the doors, when someone passed me going out to the parking lot. For some reason, I turned around to watch, and realized it was my high school boyfriend from 40 years ago. I immediately recognized his walk, and he was walking towards a car with MO plates. I yelled his name and he turned around. Knowing without a doubt it was him, I walked over and we stood outside talking for 45 minutes.

It was so good to see him. He was my first love, so it was wonderful that I was able to see him after all these years. We hugged goodbye, and the months following I kept asking myself why this happened. Almost a year later, I found out. He suddenly died of an aneurysm. I was devastated, but all I kept thinking was that this boy was such an important part of my life, and God gave me the chance to say goodbye to him. I felt blessed for that.

From an Appreciative Flight Attendant

During a very dark period of my life at the age of 50, my husband walked out, my mother died, and I was forced to sell my home. I was devastated, and said a prayer asking God if He was closing one door in my life that he would open another.

I had always wanted to be a flight attendant when I was younger but I married and had a family so I had given up the idea. On January 1st, 1992, I wrote on a napkin a New Year's Resolution that I would become a flight attendant. I opened the morning newspaper two days later and read that Northwest Airlines was interviewing for flight attendants at a local hotel. I didn't really think that they would hire me at my age, but decided to go anyway and make them tell me no. To my surprise, they hired me on the spot, and two days later I was in Minneapolis training to be a flight attendant. For the next fifteen years I traveled all over the world and lived the last ten years of my career in Hawaii. There is a God and miracles do happen... Einstein was wrong.

From a Stranded Motorist

Years ago, I was working third shift and it was the dead of winter, with one of the coldest nights on record. I had a beater of car, and little did I know that I had not properly prepared it for that kind of cold. The water in my engine had frozen as I worked my shift. While I could start the car, there was no fluid flowing through the engine. I left from work about 4 AM. No one is on the road at that time. I got about a mile before I was pegging the temperature gauge for a very hot engine. I pulled over because I knew I would only damage the car. I was not properly prepared for any kind of walk in the frigid cold. I did get out, popped the hood, and looked at the frozen water in the radiator. I did not know what to do.

This guy suddenly appears next to me, asking if he can help in any way. I did not hear him drive up or see headlights. Nothing. Thinking no way possible that he might have some anti-freeze, I asked anyway. He said "Sure, I have some in the trunk". We poured the anti-freeze in and kept the engine running on idle which slowly melted the water. The water broke free and I was able to drive home. I was just in disbelief. There could not have been a greater time of need, when out of nowhere this man 'angel' coincidentally was at the same place as me... stopped... and had anti-freeze? Wow. I gave him what I had in my wallet... $20 and cautiously went home. Never got his name and quite honestly I can't remember his face. But that incident is forever burned into my memory.

From a Doting Dad

My daughter, Olivia, graduated from Mizzou in 2009. In February of that year, she called me while I was driving home from work to tell me she had decided to go to Africa after graduation on a mission trip. She had already taken some short trips to Central America, but she was thinking about spending a year or so this time. I nearly drove off the road.

My wife and I supported her, but of course we had some trepidation. Olivia wasn't sure where she was going to go or what she was going to do, so she started searching the Internet and asking her church friends. I also sent an e-mail around my office asking if anyone had a relative or close friend who had been to Africa on a longer term mission trip. One of the responses I got was from one of my partners, who also happens to live in my subdivision; he said his sister, Lynn, had been living and working for several years in a small and very poor country in West Africa called Burkina Faso. She had already built two schools in small villages where there were none, and was training the locals how to teach. Her organization is called Burkina Faso Outreach.

Shortly after that, before I could even tell my wife about Lynn, my daughter called me at the office and said she had been told by someone about a woman who was opening schools and training teachers in a country called Burkina Faso. The woman's name, she said, was Lynn Peters. I asked her if she knew who Lynn Peters was. She said all she had was a name. I told her about my conversation with Lynn's brother, and she responded in an incredulous tone of voice, "You mean I babysat for Lynn Peters' nephews and niece?"

Now, we are talking big major coincidence here. There were many more along the way as Olivia started raising funds for her trip. It seemed that whenever she mentioned she was going to Africa, people would ask her where she was going to go. Whenever she mentioned Lynn's name and Burkina Faso Outreach, so many people said they knew Lynn and were supporting her financially (including Olivia's dentist).

The deal was sealed in our hearts and minds just a few weeks before Olivia was to leave for Burkina Faso. Even though my wife and I were secure in our faith that she would be safe, we naturally had a small thought in the back of our minds about the uncertainties of life in a poor African country. My wife was going through some old pictures when one in particular caught her eye. She rushed upstairs from the basement to show me. Neither of us (nor Olivia) had any recollection of this, but when Olivia was in elementary school, she had participated in a "model UN" project in 4th or 5th grade which was intended to help the children get some insight into other countries and cultures. The picture showed Olivia with a sign identifying the country she had selected to learn about: Burkina Faso. Now that's what I call a coincidence. Actually it was more than that, it was a message from God that he had a plan for Olivia and was watching over her. All of our hesitation vanished.

Appendix B

Google "evidence for historical Jesus," and you will get a mixed bag of results. Firm atheist and firm believer will firmly see different things. For every argument one way, there's a counter-argument.

This is not surprising. There was no mass communication or social media in the first century. Palestine wasn't the center of the known universe; Rome was. Also, Christianity didn't just take off like a rocket when his followers claimed he rose from the dead. It was more like a slow burn that gradually grew hotter and hotter.

The Biblical evidence is subjective, not objective. It comes from a faith perspective, not a straight "just the facts" one. This is why you have differing takes on Jesus within the Gospels. Luke is the one with the nativity story, and interprets Jesus for the Gentiles. Matthew is the one with the three wise men and interprets Jesus for the Jews. Mark dispenses with a birth story at all, as if he didn't know one, and goes straight to Jesus' mission and message. John focuses upon him being divine.

Over 200 years ago, some folks started a "quest for the historical Jesus." That's another good Google search. They tried to find the historical man the Gospel writers wrote about in theological terms. If Jesus existed, who was he, and what did he say? Recent examples include the Jesus Seminar and a work referred to earlier, *Zealot: The Life and Times of Jesus of Nazareth*, by Reza Aslan.

The criticism of such work is that many people who sought a "historical Jesus" ended up depicting him according to their own biases.

It's admirable to do due diligence trying to find historical evidence to substantiate your faith in Jesus or your lack of faith in him. But maybe trying to find objectivity for a subjective relationship is counter-intuitive.

Questions for Reflection and Discussion

Chapter One—Where Atheists Are Right

For believers:

What are your assumptions about people who don't believe, and what do you base them on?

Is it possible to live a good, moral life without belief in God? Why?

How would you respond to the reasons atheists have for non-belief?

For non-believers:

What are your reasons for non-belief?

How would you respond to the reasons for non-belief given in this chapter? Agree, disagree? Add to? Why?

What stereotypes do you have of believers? What do you base them on?

Chapter Two—Where Fundamentalists Are Right

For believers:

If you are a Christian, in which of Borg's categories do you see yourself?

It's been said, "You'll always lose an argument with a fundamentalist." Why?

How would you reconcile some of the things we find in the Bible with learnings from science and other disciplines?

For non-believers:

What Christians do you know, and how do they compare to the fundamentalist Christians?

Why do you think they hold so tightly to beliefs that, for you, may seem illogical?

What kind of common ground would there need to be in order to hold a productive conversation with them?

Chapter Three—Connecting Atheists and Fundamentalists

Do you agree or disagree that both believer and non-believer are more alike than different? Why?

In what ways does your belief or non-belief system give you security?

If you were to write a one paragraph summary of the story your brain creates, telling you what are "true" thoughts and actions, what would it say?

Chapter Four—You Aren't Who You Think You Are

What examples can you give where your brain on autopilot, on your behalf?

What did you used to think was true, but you're now not sure of anymore? What caused the change?

If there are over 7 billion people in the world, each with 7 billion outlooks on life, how can we determine what is true or not?

By the way, what *is* truth, anyway?

Chapter Five—God Isn't Who You Think God Is

For believers:

Which version of God are you most comfortable with? Where are places in the Bible that present a different view? How do you reconcile those views?

If you were Job, what would you want to ask God, and how do you think God would answer?

For non-believers:

Which version of God is easiest to believe, if you were to believe: the intimate or the distant? Why?

By the way the Book of Job ends, what does that say about the problem of pain in the world, such as why bad things happen to good people?

Chapter Six—The Bible Isn't What You Think It Is

For believers:

Given the objections non-believers may have regarding the Bible, why is it important to you?

How do you deal with strange stories or harsh teachings?

For non-believers:

What is the popular appeal of a book that seems ancient and irrelevant?

What can you gain from this book, even if you don't think it's inspired?

Chapter Seven—Honesty and Humility

What characteristics describe an honest person? A humble one?

What is the relationship between honesty and humility, on the one hand, and your faith, or your outlook on life, on the other?

What things do you encounter that encourage dishonesty and pride? How do you deal with them?

Chapter Eight—Transcendence and Gratitude

What would your definition of transcendence be?

What transcendent moments come to mind for you?

Simply considering what it means to be a human living in this world, for what are you grateful?

Chapter Nine—Mystery: A Collection of Truly Strange Events

How do you explain these events?

Why would you want to explain them?

What events may you have had that seem strange?

How much of all this is seeing what you want to see, and what may be objective fact? Does it matter? Why or why not?

What transcendent moments come to mind for you?

Simply considering what it means to be a human living in this world, for what are you grateful?

Chapter Ten—Jesus Isn't Who You Think He Is

Why are people fascinated by Jesus?

In what ways does Jesus impact you if you don't believe in him as the "Son of God?"

In what ways does he impact you if you do?

What's the difference? Why?

Chapter Eleven—Faith Isn't What You Think It Is

How would you define faith?

Do you have to believe in God to have faith?

How are curiosity and faith linked?

Chapter Twelve—The Church Isn't What You Think It Is

How has a faith/non-faith community helped shape your worldview?

How has it hindered it?

What would the ideal faith/non-faith community look like for you?

Chapter Thirteen—A Different Take on the Bible

Does something literally need to have happened in order for it to be "true?"

How would you decide which Biblical laws to follow, and which not?

What other questions would you ask in order to get meaning from a passage?

Chapter Fourteen—A Different Vision

What do you think it means to say that the line between sincere believer and sincere non-believer is very thin?

Do we have to be a professed Christian in order to relate to Christ? Why?

What will you take with you from reading this book?